THE WOUNDED SHAMAN:
Confronting The Darkness

A Fifth Book By:

Karen Degenhart, MA, MDiv. PhD.

Aka: Thunder Stone Dream Woman,
Ravenwolf, & Morningstar

THE WOUNDED SHAMAN:
CONFRONTING THE DARKNESS
A Fifth Book By Karen Degenhart
ISBN: 978-0-916337-05-6
© Karen Sue Degenhart, April, 2007.

No Library of Congress Number assigned. Degenhart, Karen, January 9, 1954 - Shamanism, Autobiography, Non-fiction.

First Published at Café Press, with the assistance of Mark A. Valco. Thunderbird Publications, a Division of Karnak, Enterprises, LLC. is the publisher of origin, owned by Karen Degenhart, Idaho Springs, CO. 80452.
Copies are available from http:/createspace.com/3332323. To see how to order Karen's other books, please see the two last pages of this book. Karen also has a website at http://karendegenhart.com.

This book is dedicated to my friend, Mark A. Valco, who did so much to put this book together, and get it on CreateSpace for me. Mark has a book available at http://cafepress.com/wary and also at http://createspace.com/3333979 and also at http://createspace.com/3334531. Photo on cover is Karen's funeral bed.

INTRODUCTION:

This book is a continuation of the Shamanic Journeys and inner process from my previous book, MEDICINE JOURNEYS: A SHAMANIC DESTINY. At some point in the future, I may combine them into one book. But, for now, this is the surprising true ending of this real life story of Shamanic training in what is basically called Core Shamanism, with an experienced Shamanic Guide. His regular job was as a Psychiatriac Nurse, but in his free time he became the center of a community, which was almost cult-like in some ways. While being a small built 56 year old man with a ponytail, who was of Apache, Hopi and I think Mexican descent, a very quiet and reserved person, he still had some strange effect on women. He led people into the depths of their souls--in fact, he had been given the name "Awakens Many Souls", by one of his mentors. And yet, over time I discovered that he sometimes misused his magnetic attraction, and his ability to stir the soul depths of others, into inappropriate relationships.

Most of this book was written at the time it occurred, or very recently after events occurred, so there is a journal style to the writing, and sometimes I may repeat myself, as I process the odd experiences and information that come to light. Perhaps one day I will edit it down, but for now, I think this captures more of my process in this experience to leave it as it was originally written. The last few pages were written six years later, to conclude the story. It took me that long to let go of some of the trauma which this experience-- and some similar ones-- left with me. Now I am ready to move ahead to a new phase of my life, where I can begin to USE the teachings and insights I had gained from my shamanic training and experiences.

3

The Shaman does indeed go through torture, dismemberment, betrayal, death and rebirth to become a true Shaman. It is not an easy path, and yet the lessons are unforgettable. After it is all over, the soul reaps many rewards.

While this is the conclusion of my work with the Shaman in my previous book, there will of necessity be another book following this one that fills in some other details of my Shamanic process.

This first chapter jumps right into the Shamanic Journey process, and is somewhat technical in recording history that I discovered which corroborates some objective reality about my journey, almost as if it was a Remote Viewing of the past. Be patient with this part, and if it goes too slowly, skim over it and move faster to the next chapter. It will all fall in place. (April 2, 2007)

CHAPTER ONE:
JOURNEY ELEVEN: TRAUMA IN PERU

In my last journey, which finished up my previous book, I had found a place of Sanctuary or resolution after a period of many changes, being out of work on and off for months, and breaking up with my boyfriend of nine years.   As this book begins, I am still friends with my former boyfriend, but we are both keeping our options open to date others. That is a balancing act sometimes for me, but so far the new freedom has given me more time to focus on what I really want to do, and allowed me to flex my spiritual muscles with out wondering how it will affect our relationship. The down side of my current situation is that, thought I have a new and better job, it also has a terrible schedule for socializing, meeting new people, and doing some of the shamanic work I want to be doing. I financially need my current job for now, but I do hope that one day I can make a living doing something even more stimulating, or more in line with my higher purposes.

As I entered into a shamanic journey with my Shaman friend guiding me, I had been thinking of finding a way to visit Machu Picchu in Peru. I had found a company which would offer a mostly free tour if one could recruit eight paying customers into it. So, after doing the special breathing, and getting through the relaxation induction, all I could do for a while was ruminate and try to ask Spirit for help in areas I was thinking about. I wanted to experience more of Peru, especially Machu Picchu, and I wanted to know more about where I might have known Antonio before, in other lifetimes, or where ever. I felt I had not gotten to the bottom of that question yet. In any case, I felt close to my teacher, and still felt it was beyond the meaning of an ordinary relationship.

Finally, the journey seemed to get in gear, when I walked up some stone steps in a narrow hallway, and found myself walking around at Machu Picchu. I imagined the possibility that I could be a speaker or tour leader there someday, and sell copies of my previous book, as part of it. I saw I had a copy of this book in my hands: MEDICINE JOURNEYS: A SHAMANIC DESTINY. In actuality, it is still at the printer, but I had just chosen the cover paper, so I knew kind of how it would look. As I walked around there, I still felt kind of alone, as even with all the great stuff of being at Machu Picchu, and having a book out, and so on, I still did not have a special life partner to share all this with. In a sense, even my victories were empty in that respect. While I knew I was with a tour, and even possibly a speaker for this one, I walked off alone for a while to explore this feeling of being empty and alone. Suddenly, I was taken to another time and place where this alone feeling emerged even stronger. By following the feeling, I was led deeper into my shamanic journey.

Then, it was as if I were looking up to a higher ledge where I saw a leader of Machu Picchu standing above me. He was tall, and wore a ceremonial outfit with a tunic of red down the middle, and had a sun-circle on his breast.. It also had some other layers under that, maybe of purple, turquoise, with white as the bottom garment. Because of the bright colors, I realized he easily could have been the person to have worn the red and turquoise moccasins I had seen in the dream that had led me to the shaman, Antonio, who became my mentor and guide. Somehow I also knew that only the Incan leaders had such colorful clothing, or at least, that colorful moccasins like that were only worn for ceremony, but that more practical sandals were worn most other times.

I saw this King or leader, and then all the sudden, I went into him, and I felt what he felt. I sort of became him, and went into his time. I knew his story, and that this alone feeling I was having at Machu Picchu, while it was initiated by my own feelings, was also something much worse, and more ancient than my own feelings. I started to cry some, and tears came down the side of my face. I entered into a time when bad people came to Peru, and basically killed off, tortured, and took away as slaves the people who lived there. The main idea being that now all of this leader's people were gone, but he was left alone, alive!

The bad people were trying to get him to reveal where he, or the people, had hidden the gold relics. The leader just could not reveal that. This treasure had been hidden in a tunnel, with lots of gold objects, like a golden disk, and some ancient gold plates with a mysterious, sacred writing on them that told about ancient times from the beginnings on this planet. The writing had a lot of indents and triangles in it, molded into the gold plates, I could see.

I felt that I was experiencing his pain. I felt that he had a brother who sort of ruled or co-ruled another Provence, and that the bad people had captured this brother and killed him right in front of the leader, to get him to reveal the secret hiding place of the treasure. I felt this was Inca, or even pre-Incan, and in my notes I found that I had written the dates of 1200–1230AD as a possible date for this. But, I was not totally sure that it was not also possibly 1200BC, or even 12,000BC, to translate it into our own time line.

There were just NO PEOPLE! They were killed or taken somewhere, and he had no one left, but the king could not reveal where the treasure and the gold plates with the ancient writing were hidden. Then I saw that there was a tree, a short, crooked tree, near the entrance to the tunnel at that time. There was a chance that a few of the women and children had escaped through the tunnel where the gold was hidden.

I felt that the brother who was killed may well have been Antonio, my shaman friend now. I felt it was possible that I

7

knew Antonio from this time, and that was also why we worked together so well on a different level now. I felt sometimes protective of Antonio, which fit my first journey session, in which he was my son in one life, and now in this one I felt he could have been my younger brother.

I also sometimes got the feeling that Antonio had once been kind of high up in the Church, like a Cardinal, or something. But, I also kept getting a hanging associated with the Cardinal idea, as if someone had been hung for being a heretic, and he felt badly that he some how could not intervene and prevent it. There were bad people in the Church who wanted to persecute certain people and groups. He vowed never to be a part of that kind of thing again. He may have some relationships in his life with people who he could not save then, who he has had to deal with or save this time, because he missed his chance then, more by a sin of omission than commission. Guilt by association, so to speak. Or a sincere desire to correct a wrong, voluntarily, more than as a karmic debt. These are just insights I got about my teacher, that came up briefly in this journey, at some point, because I had asked Spirit to learn more about my teacher's lives.

As I got more into the journey, it became an emotional venting or release kind of experience, and not so much seeing scenes or content. I just wailed and cried and screamed and moaned and wimpered in various ways for a long time. I lost control of it, and it seemed I could not wind down or stop. I was experiencing the horror of the destruction of a civilization, and a people. I was feeling the horror of the leader to be left alone, and not be able to protect them at all, but only to give his life to protect the secret treasure.

I felt that the leader finally submitted, and offered his neck to them, and they decapitated him. But, death did not bring peace, and my moaning and crying went on and on. Finally, Antonio had to stop drumming and come by me with calming

8

energy to help me come out of it. I took his hand and gradually could detach enough to stop and tell some of the story, as I laid there. It was just too much--to have no people left, and be left alive. Yet, it was a theme that had come up for me before, in other journeys, and in one past life reading.

As I came out of it, I could joke some, and admit that it seems real when I am in it, and yet hard to believe when I am back out of it.

Antonio told me to burn a candle as I slept during the night. And he wanted me to write up this journey, which is now the beginning of my fifth book.

During this journey I also got the word, "Wiraquocha," which I had already heard was the Andean word for God, by reading the book INITIATION: A Woman's Spiritual Adventure in the Heart of the Andes, by Elizabeth B. Jenkins. (Putnam, NY., 1997.) And, in fact, I also had been looking into tours given by her group, the Wiraqocha Foundation, but felt I was instead, for now, being guided to try another company that offered a way to earn a mostly free or discounted trip, by recruiting others for the trip. Still, there is a Wiraqocha Temple, which made me think there was a chance that my intense experience was not taking place at Machu Picchu, but could have been at other Peruvian locations, during the same time period.

I was exhausted the next day, but luckily was off work another day. I went to the library to order some books on Inca history, so that I might see what this experience could possibly be talking about. It could also be a symbolic way for me to work out some of my own issues. Still, I suspect they are issues that have come up in more than one of my lifetimes, so this symbolism is as good as any. 4/25/01

REFLECTIONS AFTER RESEARCH:

While my Journey started at Machu Picchu, when I did

some research on Peruvian history, I found out that the Spanish had never found Machu Picchu. It was not discovered until July 24, 1911 by Hiram Bingham. (Pg. 482, Hemming, John THE CONQUEST OF THE INCAS, Harcourt, Brace, Jonanovich, New York, 1970.) My own impressions of my journey was that the tall man I saw supposedly "at" Machu Picchu was a spirit who was still guarding the place, who was sad that it was no longer inhabited by his people. I felt that he was taller than the usual Peruvians, but that could be from looking up at him from a lower position, or also could be because he was a spirit, as spirits are sometimes larger than people are, especially if they are powerful spirits. I know this because at a Sundance once I sensed some HUGE spirits leading the Sundance procession, and they were about 12 to 15 feet tall, at least. The other thing is that maybe a different, taller race did inhabit Machu Picchu once, even before the Incas. Maybe some older race built Machu Picchu. I have not yet done enough research to determine some of these details.

Another thing I found out was that the Incas did not have a written language. Unless, perhaps there was some hidden knowledge that only a few knew about, so the golden tablets I saw hidden in a tunnel or cave were possibly more ancient, from Lumeria, or some other ancient time.

There was one really big thing I found out from researching this Journey session experience, and that is that the last Inca ruler was executed by the Spanish, or in particular by one man, Dr. Loarte, working for Toledo, who was out to get rid of all the Inca leaders. This last Inca ruler was named Tupac Amaru, which means Royal Serpent. (Pg. 419, Hemming.) And he was killed by beheading! That was one detail that I was sure of in my vision. I told Antonio, that I felt that I was this Inca king who was beheaded, as I experienced the journey. This is unique, as Tupac's "captains" were hung, instead. The beheading was supposed to be more dignified.

10

Then, there is the detail about the spirit I saw wearing a red tunic, or outer covering. In Hemming's book, (pg. 441) it says that Tupac Amaru, when captured, was wearing "a mantle and tunic of crimson velvet, and his shoes were of a local wool in various colours. The crown or headdress called mascapiacha was on his head, with a fringe over his forehead, these being the royal insignia of the Inca.." And, as for the sun design over his breast, Mark Amaru Pinkham, in his book, THE RETURN OF THE SERPENTS OF WISDOM , Adventures Unlimited Press, Kempton, Illinois, 1997, page 58, says that Tupac Amaru wore the medallion of the Paititi Secret Society, connected with the Solar Brotherhood, which one would guess might be some kind of Sun symbol.

I forgot to write in my first account that I did see a kind of tall headdress, that he wore. And a staff with feathers. The colored shoes reminded me of the colored moccasins that I saw in the dream that led me to the Shaman, Antonio.

Tupac Amaru had two brothers who ruled before him. Manco Capac was the father of three sons, Sayri Tupac, Titu Cusi, and Tupac Amaru. Manco was trying to reestablish Inca way of life. His sons ruled in succession. First Sayri, who was poisoned in 1560. Then, Titu Cusi proclaimed himself Inca (ruler), and High Priest of the Sun. Titu was only a child when his father, Manco Capac was "assassinated in front of his son's eyes." (Pg. 159, Metraux, Alfred, THE HISTORY OF THE INCAS, Random House, N.Y., 1969.) This parallels the sense I had in my Journey that someone had their close family killed in front of them. This actually happened to Titu, the younger brother of Tupac Amaru. Titu tried to make concessions with the Spanish, and even converted to Christianity (to some extent) and tried to make a peace between the Incas and the Spanish. He was baptized with the name of Philip. That only worked up to a point. Titu fell ill suddenly. A friendly Augustinian monk named Father Diego Ortiz tried to help him with prayers and medicine, but when that failed, the monk was tortured to death by some Indians. (Pg. 160,161, Metraux.)

When Titu Cusi had proclaimed himself Inca (top ruler), he had relegated his brother Tupac Amaru to the priesthood, so Tupac Amaru had been living in the monestary of the Virgins of the Sun. When Titu died suddenly (possibly from poison), the captains and generals called Tupac Amaru to be the new Inca king. (Pg. 419, Hemming; pg. 161, Metraux.)

Consulting Metraux, I found out that Tupac Amaru was the oldest son, but that he did not seem to have the qualities of a leader or general, thus the father (strangely called Pachacuti in this book, not Manco Capac), first chose the younger brothers to be his heir. It was only after the first chosen sons were killed that the generals resorted to making Tapac Amaru the Incan leader. (Pg. 85, Metraux.)

I admit that I was at first confused when I found out that Tupac Amaru was not allowed to take the leadership, as in my journey I felt he was the oldest. But, I was vindicated in my insight when I read that it was because he did not seem to be the type for that role that he was saved for last choice.

Tupac Amaru's deceased brother, Titu Cusi, had been very into the theatrical, and would wear masks and elaborate outfits to impress the people, or his enemeis. (Pg. 160, Metraux.) So, it was only fitting that his funeral was the last traditional ceremony for an Inca ruler, complete with the red fringe, mace, parasol, and golden ornaments. (Pg. 161, Matraux.)

After the torture of Father Ortiz, Toledo wanted to blame all Inca rulers, and was out to get Tupac Amaru. Toledo also wanted to blame all Inca rulers for some earlier raids and fighting. Tupac Amaru was captured as he and his wife sat by a camp fire warming themselves. They had not gotten far enough into the jungle to escape. There were always some Indians of different tribes who would side with and help the Spanish, and that is how they were found in the dense jungle. When found, they were promised they would not be ill treated, so Tupac Amaru surrendered to the Spaniards. (Pg. 439, Hemming.) He was with other Indians, his wife, a governor, other captains, and wives and children.... (Pg. 440. Hemming.) Tupac Amaru was described as "affable, well-disposed, and discrete, eloquent and intelligent." (Pg. 440, Hemming.)

Tupac Amaru was put in prison, and there quickly indoctrinated into Christianity by some monks and clerics who spoke Quechua well. He was eager to learn this religion now, as he felt it might help his position to convert, and also perhaps he saw the power in those who followed Christianity. In three days he knew enough to be baptized in prison, and then he took the Christian name Pedro. (Pg. 443, Hemming.)

While they were converting and indoctrinating Tupac Amaru into Catholic Christianity, there was a speedy and unfair trial meant to blame him personally for things that had happened previously, including the death of the monk, and various murders by lynch mobs not under his control. (Pg. 445, Hemming.) "After only three days of sham trial Dr. Loarte sentenced the Inca Tupac Amaru to death. He spared him the indignity of the gallows, and decreed that he be beheaded." (Pg.446, Hemming.) Many Spanish as well as Church leaders tried to show that Tupac Armaru was innocent, and begged tearfully on their knees, that he be spared. But Viceroy Toledo refused to consider their appeals. (Pg. 447, Hemming.)

There was a gigantic crowd as he was led into the town square in Cusco, in front of the Cathedral, to his execution. There were horrible cries and wailing from all the people. Suddenly he raised a hand to signal that he had something to say, and there was silence. Then he made a speech in his language in which he said especially to his chiefs, "Lords, you are here from all the four suyos. Be it known to you that I am a Christian, they have baptised me and I wish to die under the law of God. And I have to die." Then he denounced his religion of worshiping nature and of listening to the priests who got divination from the Sun Disk, as he said it was not genuine! (Pg. 448, Hemming.) Even Toledo was surprised and glad at this confession.

Metraux also quoted some first hand account. In response to the crowds of grieving people, natives, Churchmen and Spanish alike, Tupac Amaru "...raised his right hand in a noble gesture and let it fall. All this noise was followed by a silence so profound that there cannot have been a living soul among all the people in the square, or near it, who moved. The Inca spoke with an eloquence unusual in a man about to die. He said his life had run its course and he deserved his fate. He implored all those who had children never to curse them for any bad behavior, but only to punish them; for once as a child, he had annoyed his mother. She had cursed him and prophesied he would die by execution and not from natural causes. And now that was coming true. Fathers Carrera and Fernandez contradicted him and explained that his fate came from the will of God, and not from a mother's curse. Of this they were able to convince him, for they had the eloquence of St. Paul. The Inca repented of his words. He asked everyone to forgive him, and told the viceroy and magistrate that he would pray to God for them. The Bishop of Popoyan, don Augustin de la Coruna, and some other priests hastened to the viceroy to implore him to spare the Inca's life. They urged he be sent to Spain to be tried by the king himself. Nothing would move Don Francisco Toledo. He send Juan de Soto, a law officer of the court and a servant of the viceroy, on horseback wielding a staff to clear his passage. He galloped up furiously, his horse crushing many people. He gave the order to cut off the Inca's head at once. The Inca, having received the last rites from the priests, put his head on the block like a lamb. The executioner came forward; taking the hair in his left hand, he cut off the head with a single stroke and raised it for the crowd to see. The moment the head was struck off all the cathedral bells were rung and the bells of all the monasteries and churches in the town. The execution caused the greatest sorrow and brought tears to everyone's eyes. The head was impaled on the point of a lance, near the scaffold. It became more beautiful every day, for the Inca had been a handsome man. At night the Indians would come to adore the head, until one morning, at dawn. Juan de Sierra by chance went to his window and saw this idolatrous worship indulged in by the people. The viceroy was informed. He had the head buried with the body in one of the cathedral chapels. A pontifical mass was sung for the repose of the Inca's soul and all the clergy of the town took part in the funeral. Numerous masses, with organ music, were said in his honor, for he had been a great lord and an Inca." (Pg. 161,162, Metraux, THE HISTORY OF THE INCAS, Random House, N.Y. 1969.) This is quoted from some source not clearly mentioned in the text.

While Tupac Amaru had earlier allowed the revival of the Inca beliefs, now at his death he upheld the validity of Christianity. It seemed as if he had betrayed his people and culture. But,there were some beliefs that by our standards were a bit odd. They would mummify their former kings, for example, and bring their mummified bodies out to be worshiped and receive offerings from time to time. The priests tried to get the people to bury these mummified bodies, and they would not leave them in the graves, but would still dig them up from time to time so that they would not have the weight of the earth upon them. (Pg. 72, Metraux.) There were also special stones that protected a village, which were buried in a secret place and then taken out periodically to have offerings made to them. (Pg. 73, Metraux.)

These kinds of things, might be considered superstitious by the priests. Oddly enough, today we are going back to finding some value, or a different understanding, of the psychological value of these kinds of symbolic rituals. We can see them from a new level, after having had a more "scientific" mind set previously. It is strange how things come around full circle. Now, today the citizens of the Christian world are becoming more interested in the primitive beliefs and cultures, as well as their spiritual and shamanic teachings. But we see it all from a new level, where we have the "modern" objectivity, as well as the belief in the power of ancient ceremony or ritual. 5/2/01

Oddly enough, this story brought up issues for me, so that it seems to fit me in a way. I feel at a deep level that one has to be Christian first, and then one is free to explore shamanism or wicca, or to incorporate Jungian psychology into ones belief system or practice. In other words, if one has never been Christian, I am suspicious or not as sure of a person's spiritual integrity, but if they are a renegade Christian, they can do what ever they want, as they have the Holy Spirit in them, still. 5/3/01

My reading also told me that relocation of peoples who were not conforming to new rule was common. This was a method that Incas themselves used on those they conquered, and then the Spanish used it on them as well. So, when the Inca spirit, who I "went in to" felt badly because his people were gone, there is a possibility that some leader, chief or noble, not necessarily the top ruler, had this happen to him, that his subjects that he had ruled or supervised were moved, leaving him with no one. That idea and feeling of not having any people left could come from a relocation of some group of people.

On the other hand, from the psychological view point, it could be how a part of me feels, as I have "no people" around me. My mother and siblings live in Australia, and I have only a handful of other relatives living in Illinois or Indiana, who I rarely see anymore. My dad and stepmother are dead. And my boyfriend of nine years, has been trying to date other women. When he fails to find anyone new, he tries to win me over again, but now I am not interested in anything too serious, as I have wasted so much of my life on him already. Still, there is some connection that we can't seem to let go of, and that still confuses me. While he seems to be attracted to every woman, I am rarely attracted to any men, as I am more particular. I wonder if there will ever be someone new , who is also available and interested in me, who I like enough. The spiritual qualities I desire and the understanding of me and my work are hard to find. And then they have to like me, too, so who knows if that will ever happen? That is why I have kept going back to my X-boyfriend over the years, as he was still sort of pursuing me. He never gives me enough time and space to find someone new, even when he wants to break up with me. I guess this issue is not resolved for me yet. I am honest about it, since my shamanic journeys are also therapeutic, and dealing with my issues, as well as somehow tuning in on past lives or akashic records of past history.

I truly do not know for sure if I was once Tupac Amaru, but I do believe I have been doing at least a kind of historical Remote Viewing, in this last Journey session experience. 05/06/01

As far as the date I felt I picked up from my journey, one book (Metraux, pg. 200) says that the year 1200AD is the "Beginnings of Inca civilization and state, as well as the kingdom of the Chimus, successors of Mochicas." The dates of 1200BC. Or 12.000BC might relate to some earlier civilization. Particularly the 12,000BC might relate to some kind of refugees from Atlantis or the remains of MU. But, it is an interesting synchronicity that the 1200 AD date is about when the Inca Empire started, since my journey vision was when it ended.

Just for some perspective, here is a time line of some other dates that fit my story: "Pizarro lands at Tumbez and discovers the Inca empire. 1527." "Execution of Atahuallpa, August 29" in 1533. "The Spaniards enter Cuzco. Nov. 15, 1533." "Revolt of

17

Manco Capac II, and siege of Cuzco, 1536." "Manco Capac takes refuge in the mountains of Vilcabamba and there founds a new Inca state. 1537." "Manco Capac assassinated by the Spaniards. 1545." (These from page 200, of Metraus' book, THE HISTORY OF THE INCAS.) "Reign of his son, who submits in 1555. 1545-1560." "Reign of Titu Cusi at Vilcabamba. 1560-1571." "The Spaniards conquer Vilcabamba, capture the Inca Tupac Amaru, and execute him. 1572." "The orders of the viceroy Francisco de Toledo take effect, giving Peru a new political and social structure. 1572." (Pg. 201, Metraux.) I am not sure what all of this means, but it gives some idea of the time in history that my vision is talking about.

The Shaman wrote in an e-mail that he did not identify with this story, or the Catholic Cardinal idea, from his own journey work, but I could be tuning in on something I need to know about, even if he was not involved as a player in these scenarios. Or, maybe he just is not supposed to know this. It is still odd that I felt I was his older brother, and that Tupac Amaru was the oldest. And that his younger brother, Titu Cusi did witness the execution of his father as a child. The themes and details are still close to my vision, even if the soul of my Shaman friend, Antonio, is not the real brother to the me as Tupac Amaru. I might not have been Tupac Amaru, either, but this story could have come through as a teaching for me to know more about Peruvian history for when I go there. This does make history come alive, that is for sure.

I am sure there is more for me to learn about the history of Peru, but for now, this will do. Another insight I got from this is that Tupac Amaru, though it seemed that he betrayed his own people's religion by converting to Catholicism, was really doing the right thing in that by doing so, he could help the people conform to the new religion and new rule by the Spanish easier, so that they would not be slaughtered and politically persecuted as much. He might have seen that he had to do this to help save his people from more suffering, that would come if they were to resist too much. So, he may have been more politically sly than it appeared. 5/08/01

By the end of this chapter, my job is changing to the overnight shift. I can bring things to read, and maybe even do some writing at work, as long as I can stay awake. And I will have more flexibility to see clients or go to meetings in the evenings before work. This can be an important change for me. 05/10/01

After a couple of weeks, I had to return the library books on Peru that I had taken out. But, the more I read, the more my clues from the journey were accurate. For example, there was the word "Wiracocha," the Inca word for the Creator that I received. And the gold sun disk that Tupac Amaru had hidden. These clues were verified when I read in ANCIENT CIVILIZATIONS OF THE ANDES (Philip Ainsworth Means, Gordian Press, N.Y. 1973) that there was a "circular or oval" plate of gold which was a statue of the sun, that "came into the hands of the Inca Tupac Amaru I," (pg. 395.) The author Means suggested that this oval disk represented a sort of combination of the Creator Viracocha, and the Sun God Inti, even though it was called Viracocha. (Pg. 396.) In other words, there was a disk called Wiracocha (by which ever spelling) that Tupac Amaru had in his possession.   There was also a Temple of Viracocha or Wiracocha, and this Temple had a Catholic Cathedral built over it. I don't have the source for that now, but read it in one of the books I was studying. It is possible that the Cathedral that Tupac Amaru was executed in front of, had been the site of the Temple of Wiracocha. That would confirm my sense of place being not necessarily at Machu Picchu, but at some place called Wiracocha, which turned out to fit, as this drama happened in Cusco, not Machu Picchu.

This story was dramatic, but I had to take a break from studying Peruvian history, so while this is still kind of sketchy

19

information, it is amazing that I got what information I did from a Shamanic Journey.

CHAPTER TWO: JOURNEY TWELVE:
DARK NIGHT OF THE SOUL
IN THE CAVERNS UNDER TEOTIHUACAN

This journey started with me viewing the Earth from space. Then I'm on the Earth. Next, I'm finding some stone steps that go underground to a cavern, that is like a tomb. It's not completely dark, as I can see that on one wall of this tomb-like room is the Mayan/Aztec Calendar Stone.

I observe a figure draped in black come into this room and sit with head bowed, and covered completely with the black cloak cloth that covers his whole body. I do not see a face at all, but it is probably a man.

The figure is sitting on a bench of some kind, head bowed, for a long, long time. The figure is me, or an entity I am assuming and experiencing.

I felt from observing this figure that there was a sense of being stuck or trapped in this tomb-like cavern, staring at the Calendar Stone on the wall, for centuries. Time just kept going on. The figure felt that he (or I?) had been dropped off on this planet aeons ago, and then abandoned here by his people, as they never came back for him. He was left on this lonely mission without hope. He wanted to "go home," in a sense to die, for he no longer felt connected to anything, and everything felt flat, and like cardboard, dry and unsatisfying.

He waited like this for centuries, until he felt that maybe they were not coming back for him, that he was completely lost and abandoned. There were no other humans or people in this story, or entering the dark place. He felt that his mind and feelings had been blocked off completely, so that even though

21

he had a vague memory of his real home and the joy of being with his people, it was not real to him now. Still, he longed to go home and forget the turmoil and pollution of this world. This world was nearly a hopeless case in our time now, he sensed. There were only pockets of relief, and little real joy—mostly experienced by the rich.

He (and I) tried to die, to stop breathing, but instead had to breathe again, after holding his (my) breath a moment. He just could not die.

I could sometimes feel this cool tingling energy come over me when I did try to "die," or perhaps to go out of body. The cool and tingling was some energy coming over my body. I remembered getting that feeling when I was six or seven years old, and that I could go into this altered state when the vacuum cleaner was being run by my Mom, from the vibrations of it. It was a kind of mystical feeling I could generate. I got that same feeling this time when I tried to hold my breath or stop breathing for a few seconds. It is a pleasurable feeling of a spiritual nature, not sexual, and was like being bathed in a cleansing, sparkling energy of lightness. It was as if, when one was in danger of dying, a spiritual energy comes to help one to recover, or pass over. Thus, I got "help" by feeling like dying....

Everything felt like a dead end now. I had broken up with my boyfriend of nine years, and he had recently been mean to me about my cats that he hated, so I knew that we could never get back together, as he hated my pets. And his dogs were always a conflict for me, as he treated them better than he treated me, and they had more rights than I did.

I had a job I was now stuck in for the money in which I worked four, ten hour overnight shifts, and this backwards style was playing with my mind and energy level, too. And it only pays $10.00 an hour.

I was also at an impasse in my relationship with Antonio, my

Shaman friend, as something seemed to have lessened in intensity from some of the energy we had been able to share etherically a few months earlier--before my book was done and my job situation stabilized. Perhaps finishing the book put some kind of an ending to a phase of our work, and yet, a new beginning had not yet really happened, either. I was still not getting steady clients for my shamanic practice, or getting the classes and groups together that I had wanted to develop. And part of the problem was having an apartment that is hard to keep neat, which is a bit too small for all the stuff I have now, and thus not open enough for meetings and groups, and even hard to have clients come to.

I knew I was not completely "done" with working with the Shaman, and I felt incomplete about my work to become a shamanic practitioner. Yet, I felt I was floundering around with it, partly because my book had been completed, and yet the book only showed the messy ness of my process and life.... It was sort of embarrassing, in a way. Even though I learned a lot from my journeys.

It seemed that I should be able to get and hold more clients if I were progressing more, but that wasn't working out.

It also seemed that I wanted to be closer friends with the Shaman, instead of only seeing him for journey sessions, but that seemed awkward, and also he provided little opportunity for this. I wondered how it was possible that he was closer friends with his former apprentice, Nancy, and even taught classes with her. Somehow, I felt inadequate, since he did not seem to have any ideas for doing classes or workshops with me. Yet, I was also still an apprentice, so perhaps I was not yet ready-even though I had so many educational degrees.....

Then some recent problems wondering how I could ever afford to live if I had to move to another apartment if I got in trouble for having my cats--when no pets were allowed in the building--weighed me down. For my current rent was very low for the Denver area.

Abandonment. I felt friendly toward the Shaman, yet slightly abandoned by him, even to see him for a journey. Something was different, now. And I felt I had been used and abandoned by my former boyfriend as well.

I felt my job was like a "non-life" job--staying awake all night, doing almost nothing, for four nights a week, just to pay my bills, making around $10.00 an hour. I did try to read and use my time, but being so tired, I was not able to do that for the whole time there.

It just seemed I was stuck and unable to make my life have any real joy or connection, anymore. I felt dead sexually, with no passion left in me for anyone. My body felt numb. I didn't feel any hope to ever be deeply connected to anyone again. I had felt connected energetically to the Shaman for a while (not physically), but that had been "switched off", too.

I felt lost. My journey only reflected my despair and my wish to die--and yet, I could not die. That is what my journeys showed me--for even in dying, my spirit lived on to be further tormented in another life time, by mistreatment, and lack of real love and joy....

My journeys were getting futile and depressing. It seemed like the longer I lived the more likely I would become a homeless old person with no stability or closeness with anyone--particularly any romantic relationship.

The figure in the cavern waited and waited, and no one ever came to get him. He wanted to go "home" to the stars again. It seemed that they were never going to come back for him. He felt he could not accomplish his mission.... He no longer even remembered who they were. It was a Dark Night of the Soul, but a calm sort of despairing, accepting sense of defeat. He could not even die--but waited for centuries for something to happen.

But, I couldn't die in front of the Shaman--I had to keep breathing there.... It was a symbolic death, not literal.

24

As I watched the Mayan/Aztec Calendar, at one point, I realized it told aeons of stories and information--more than it seemed. And I saw a "dragon" land up on the top of it for an instant. Then later an oval shape hovered in the sky above this tomb-perhaps a spaceship-yet it did not take me, either.

I saw another, deeper stairway appear behind a wall that became invisible, the wall the Calendar Stone was on. But I could not go down there, or did not find anything magical down there, either.

When I think about dying, I can feel all tingly-an ironical experience. It is a release. An energy shoots through me, as if to say, "Don't die!"

Finally toward the end, "I" was able to go above ground, right through the roof of the tomb/cavern, and it was dark outside, so I saw the stars. But I still could not ascend to them. I had to hover near this same area. That was frustrating, too, as I only wanted to be free to go back "home," to the stars.

During the journey, I definitely got the word "Teotihuacan." I could not pronounce it, but I knew that was what was meant, that place in Mexico, with the large pyramid, as I knew this journey was in Mexico.

So, when I got home, I opened up to a book I have-- ATLAS OF ANCIENT AMERICA (Coe, Snow, and Benson, authors, Facts on File, N.Y.) and looked up Teotihuacan, page 106. On this page was a photo of the Pyramid of the Sun, and this quote: "Whether this temple was actually devoted to the worship of the Sun, as Aztec tradition would have it, is unknown, but a recent discovery underneath the pyramid suggests why the pyramid was built there in the first place. This proved to be a natural cave, enlarged by the ancients into a clover-leaf-shaped chamber, and reached by a tunnel, directly beneath the very center of the pyramid. It has been suggested on ethnohistorical grounds that the earliest Teotihuacans might have viewed this as a supernatural "Place of Emergence," a kind of cave-womb from which the ancients of the tribes came." (Pg. 106.) The

25

Pyramid of the Sun is the earliest and largest ritual structure in the city, and the place were the city was founded, this book also said.

I also noticed on page 109 of the same book that it mentions a Palace of the Quetzal-Butterfly (located in the West in front of the Pyramid of the Moon) that had been completely burned and destroyed. It says this city was destroyed by flame–whether from invasion or internal insurrection.... (109)

I then remembered the word/image of Butterfly appearing briefly in my journey. So maybe there is something about the Palace of the Quetzal-Butterfly (or its destruction) that connects somehow to my journey story.

The dark cloaked man hung out in this dark place for a long time, perhaps protecting the Calendar Disk, or just grieving, or feeling guilty about something, lost and abandoned, and left behind. And he couldn't even die--sort of like a Highlander. It was a Dark Night of the Soul....

Maybe I am just depressed or defeated or let down about my life. For it seemed no one was going to come for me. I later told the Shaman, "Now that I've met you, there's nothing else to wait for." This ambiguous statement was my feeling that nothing more potent than meeting him can now come into my life, but also, in conjunction with this journey session, perhaps there is a let down knowing that I have now had the climax of my life, and the beginning excitement of this unique magical experience is over with. There is nothing more to wait for... this is it.

But, on the other hand, I did not really have him, either, just as a Shaman, not as the true friend and relationship that I longed for and really needed. I needed more than what he could give me, from somewhere, but I no longer felt I would ever get it, in this life.

At the end of the journey, the Shaman tried another drum and put a lot of healing energy into me, thus helping to bring me back from this dark place, and to feel some healing and lightness, again. But my life still felt kind of flat. All the excitement was wearing off. Yes, there was nothing else to wait for now that I had met the Shaman, but he couldn't give me what I needed to heal me and make my life whole, either. There are always some missing pieces. So it goes.

Later, he suggested I see Nancy for Rebirthing work to get out of this stuck place. I am not sure how I feel about working with someone else, too, and a woman, who is his friend, but it is something to think about. It was something to think about, but by morning I was not convinced. The Shaman had said he felt there wasn't enough "movement" in my progress, but I was skeptical if I could open up to her. And I felt badly that he saw me that way--as not having enough movement. It made me feel like I could never get to where ever it was I was supposed to get to, to be healed. No matter how much I did, there was always more to do. Somehow, I think my life will never be normal, and don't know if Rebirthing will help with that. But, who knows? I am actually a little afraid of the idea of Rebirthing. I'm not sure why. Maybe to me it seems like trying to create some artificial experience in some way. But what I have in my journeys is real.

I later remembered that there was an image of a very huge tree in my journey. It was very wide. I know there is a sacred tree somewhere in Mexico, and think this was referring to it. Later I did manage to find out from Tony Shearer's book LORD OF THE DAWN: QUETZALCOATL (Naturegraph Publishers, Inc., Happy Camp,CA. 96039, 1971) from a photograph in this book that this tree is called El Tule, or the Zapotec Tree of Life, in Oaxaca, Mexico.

I also was getting later feelings about the words Chichen Itza, a location in Mexico. There is a Temple of the Jaguars there. This could be referring back to my first journey with the Shaman, which I wrote about in my book MEDICINE JOURNEYS: A SHAMANIC DESTINY. In that journey I also had a journey in Mexico, with some kind of Mayan situation, and Jaguars. Perhaps I was coming back to the beginning of my work with him for some reason. Full circle. The next day I found out why, and also the reason for some feelings I was getting about the Shaman and my work with him became more clear. 5/ 24-25/ 2001

CHAPTER THREE:
A WEEK OF PSYCHIC ATTACKS
LEAD TO MY FUNERAL DECISION

The same week that I saw the Shaman for that last journey was a week of tests. First I had a call Sunday about having a cat (actually two) in my apartment, when no pets were allowed. Now my pets and my home were at risk. I had them for two years here, but now someone had seen a cat in the window and reported it. I was supposed to have them out by the next weekend. I freaked. My old boyfriend at first said he would take them for the Summer, but they had to stay outside all the time. And he would not really be watching out for them. I was torn about bringing them to his place, but had no other option. I was thinking of spending the night with him in the process of bringing them there, as even though we were broken up, we sometimes got together. However, I was still torn about leaving them there, as well as tired from work, and ended up not coming when I said I would Tuesday night, so he changed his mind completely about taking them even temporarily.

So, then for the rest of my days off I went driving around and making a few calls about apartments that took cats, or checking out mobile homes. But the lot rentals for even a cheap mobile home was more than I now paid for rent. Plus, I was already in debt quite a bit, partly from charging the costs of printing my last book, and buying stock with credit card checks. So, the idea of giving notice to move before June 1st was not going to work. I ended up just keeping the cats, and blocking the windows so that they could not easily sit in the windows, and be seen, but I could risk a threat of eviction by keeping them. At this point, if I were threatened with eviction, I would have to give them to a shelter, and that would break my heart, and theirs. I raised them from babies, and they have trust in me, as their owner.

In the process of this cat problem, my boyfriend, or I should say, "X"-boyfriend, at that point, was even more critical of my $10.00 an hour overnight job. The schedule of it made it even harder for me to be free, or not tired, to visit him. Yet, this was the best job I had in years, as well as now that I was on the night shift, pretty easy. I was able to read or even write like I am now with my notebook computer. He didn't have to work, because of living in his paid-for rammed earth home, but he also was quite poor, as he lived on $250. A month from a renter/room mate, who never paid the rent on time. So, he had nothing to offer me, for his home was not up to par for my taste and only had a wood stove for heat. His dogs also were allowed to sleep between us on the bed, and so forth. I had lived there for three years on and off, and painted the whole place several times at my own expense, but it never really got fixed up like it could have, if he had that as more of a priority. And he hated all my stuff, and now, he admitted to hating my cats, and the siamese one in particular. It seemed this week like a final blow to our relationship, when he admitted how much he hated my cats, and would not take them, even for awhile.

The third attack that week was totally unexpected, and came from my session with the Shaman. His comments about seeing the Re-birther, turned out to be his way of trying to refer me to someone, so that he could work on terminating our journey work together. I was pretty confused, and the next day felt panicky about what he had said, so in later e-mails I found out his real intentions. While I thought I was an Apprentice, and I knew he had worked for years with some of his apprentices, he also seemed to think of it as a therapy, and like he could just casually "refer" me to someone else, since he was trying to end all his individual work to do only group work. He basically did not have time for me, and another man who was a client, anymore. I was to be phased out, and until he clarified this, I felt I was

30

being terminated, without warning and closure. I went through several days of pain, betrayal, and confusion over this, but finally some e-mails from him helped to give me the hope that we could talk further about how to do this "termination" more appropriately. And I could have some kind of final ceremony, or even do a Funeral ceremony, if I wanted to.

Still, all this came as a shock and out of the blue, as he had only a couple weeks before been praising me for getting my book done and published, and even acted more like we could be friends, instead of just Teacher and Apprentice. So, this new "termination" attitude was sudden and a turn about, in my mind. Though I had a hunch something was up, as I was not getting the same feeling of connection that I felt earlier in the year with him. In fact, as I drove off from that last session, I wondered to myself if that would be my last journey with the Shaman. I felt a kind of flat feeling where an excitement use to be, about him.

He had made some comment about there not being enough "movement" in my case, and I was also confused and upset about that, as I thought I was an Apprentice, not a client, and though there were many parallels, I did not know he was now thinking of me in clinical terms of progress. Yet, in a session just before this one, I had just had the most remarkable session of all, in which I re-lived the execution of the last Inca Tupac Amaru. And brought back true historical details as well. And that was not good enough "movement" for him. Perhaps it was the depressing and stuck tone of this last journey that discouraged him. But I later interpreted that journey as a psychic message to myself about the feelings I had about this subtle "termination" that he was trying to force on me without actually coming out and saying it clearly at first.

While that journey seemed morbid and depressing, full of abandonment feelings and death longings, that was the true situation that was occurring! I was about to be abandoned, I was wanting to "die" and get free of being sequestered in that underground tomb, and I wanted to find my freedom in the stars. The Mayan/Aztec Calendar which I, as the character in the journey, was staring at, is a classic Mandala symbol, referring to wholeness and completion, or the need for it. At one point, a subtle **dragon** appeared to land on the top of it, and that could be a good omen as well, as that is the Shaman's symbol, as well as an archetype discussed at length in the book, THE RETURN OF THE SERPENTS OF WISDOM, by Mark Amaru Pinkham. I gave the Shaman a copy of this book for a gift for that last session.

So, while that journey seemed to show a stuck-ness or lack of movement on one level, it actually WAS showing progress, and predicted the need for me to "die," and to find wholeness, my own Dragon power, and to do a kind of death-rebirth ceremony, to get out of the tomb I was trapped in during this journey. The unconscious knows what it is doing and that journey was perfect for the circumstances. It even predicted the Shaman's efforts to "terminate" my work with him. And it foreshadowed my need for a Death-Rebirth ceremony to get out of the tomb.

I felt that an Apprentice should never be terminated, but only moved onto a higher, and even closer, relationship with the Teacher, so they could work together more as equals. I was ambivalent about what it would mean to "graduate" as a Shaman, as I did not want to lose my connection with the Shaman, as it was already so infrequent, being about once a month or less, since I met him. The ideal would be to collaborate with him in some group work, as he was already doing with his former apprentice, Nancy. In a sense, she never "Terminated" her work with him, but only graduated to a higher level of contact with him, as I saw it. But other apprentices, who were less favored, had to move on and do their work in a vacuum. I did not want to have to move into that category.

During this same week of the other psychic attack situations, and the most heavy one about the change to come in my work with the Shaman, I also had news that my mother in

Australia had a stroke! She was still recovering from being paralyzed on her right side. So, that was probably bothering me, as well. It was a week of high stress.

To make things even more confusing, I e-mailed a note to my Hopi/Mexican friend, who is a kind of spiritual leader himself, about what happened with the Shaman. Actually, my original motive was to ask for a back up place to put my cats, if the need arose, to keep from having to give them to a shelter. But I ended up mentioning how my Teacher was trying to terminate my case! That seemed a contradiction in terms, even, as I was an Apprentice, not a client, even though there were parallels in the process. The main difference in my mind was the Indian way of taking someone into your tribe, and then you are never alone again. A normal therapist does have to terminate paying clients and they might never see one another again, but the Teacher/ Apprentice relationship seemed to me to be one that should last forever, really. It is almost more than family. It can last over different life times. Thus, the use of the "referral" idea by the Shaman as a way of separating me from the work we were doing together, in his mind was a way of giving me some other support during the separation, but in reality, that just could not work. I could not go to his other apprentice, to "finish up" my process with him! That would never work. I might find a new Teacher/therapist at some point, to learn some other things, but the unique process and relationship that I had with the Shaman could never be duplicated. Not only were my journeys totally amazing and profoundly changing my matrix of reality perception, but in a way, I really loved him, though I knew he was married, and not really available. That actual love connection cannot be duplicated. And perhaps it hurt more to think that he did not feel the same way toward me, that I was now a burden to him, to see even once a month. The only consolation was that he was also forcing his man client to quit, and I soon found out in an e-mail that this man was doing a Funeral Ceremony to complete his work with the Shaman soon,

33

and I was invited to come.

But, as I had started to say, my Hopi/Mexican friend responded to my concern about being "terminated" by the Shaman with a cryptic note that also did not let me rest: "Your Shaman friend is draining you a little at a time, spirit wise. Open up your inner eyes, RavenWolf, and see that they that wish to feed at the minds and souls of those who are we, are those who have no way of ever learning to truly see. Walk carefully in this world of deceit for they are as jackals who wish only to feast at a soul of the Elohim Children. Peace and Light."

Then, after crying and being depressed for a couple days, I had to go back to work on the night shift, but due to my anxiety could not sleep before hand. I decided to go to the Denver UFO Society meeting first, and bring some of my books to sell. But I was too late to really make a decent announcement about the books, and also had to leave the meeting early to go to work.

The topic was about Benjamin Creme's promotion of the Maytreya, a new Messiah who is now supposedly in the world. The video they showed about magical crosses appearing in windows all over the world as a kind of sign, was interesting, but something about this whole story always bothered me. For one thing, it seemed like another form of Catholicism, in a way, with its miracles and odd happenings that healed people but otherwise were not easy to understand. I tried to see how that could relate to me, if I did not have a magical cross or a magical answer to a prayer based on some sign.

The Maytreya video was also depressing, as it made one look at world poverty and problems, and how it is like the possible end of the world if we do not do something ecologically and spiritually. And this Being who called himself the Messiah, that seemed strange, too. Yet, it was not impossible. It seemed like it could be some kind of mind control experiment, or something. I could not completely trust the information, and it also made my sense of reality even more strained, after my

34

problem with the Shaman, and the contradictory message from my other advisor, The Corn Farmer (the Hopi/Mexican man's given Medicine Name.)

I ended up going to an overnight shift depressed, confused, betrayed, abandoned, and now wondering if my precious Teacher was now possessed by some kind of evil force! He had been contradictory and giving mixed messages of various kinds to me for some time, and evil does use deception and confusion to work. I really had to question everything I had come to believe in about him. This did not make for an easy time for me. It was a Hall of Mirrors.

I did pressure my Shaman Teacher to clarify his motives and what was really going on, for even though he had tried to "refer" me to a woman, he did say I could still see him, but it was a sort of hesitant response, at the time. I was still suspicious, and had to keep asking him to clarify everything, until he admitted he was trying to terminate my case, in order to end up with all his individual work and spend his time on group work. Then when he e-mailed me that his other client was also terminating and doing a Funeral Ceremony in July, that clinched it for me. I had to consider doing the Funeral Ceremony, too, as I did not want to be out-done by a guy who was not even an apprentice.

And, after another day or so of answers by e-mail from the Shaman, it became clear to me that I had to let go. He was in some new phase and what ever he seemed to want earlier, he now wanted to focus more on something else. It was still kind of mind-boggling for me, as I felt with my book being done, we could be more friends, now, though I was still happy to do the journeys as I always got some powerful information or teachings from them. And I was afraid that I could not duplicate the depth of them on my own. But, the Shaman said that he did not even want friends, now, as that would drain his energy, too. Though he has plenty of people who admired him and came to visit him, he did not think of them as friends, I guess. That was strange. He was a kind of loner who somehow also had helped all these people, even reluctantly, at times.

So, by Saturday night, I came to the conclusion that I also wanted to do the Funeral Ceremony to complete my work with him, and that meant I had to pick a date for it, and my ceremony could not be combined with the other man's day (because there is only one grave in the Shaman's back yard.) I then felt a sense of peace about that, as I had resisted the idea for so long, though had been impressed with the Funeral Ceremony done by both the Shaman and his former apprentice, Nancy. I did not like the part where one had to lay out like a corpse and have people come in and say their last message to the "dead" person, as I was sure I would cry and also perhaps laugh, in the process of that, and also maybe I would have hardly any one to come to mine, who knew me very well. I did not have a lot of friends, and I only had minimal contact with the "community" that had formerly formed around the Shaman when in years past he had more meetings at his home--meetings that were also now terminated for his new more hermit-like life. I had come almost too late to work with him at all, and only was able to attend three drumming parties at his home, before they were canceled. The fact I was able to see him at all was a miracle, but it was still hard to have to take the crumbs of what was left of a once thriving community and of what time he had left for me during the year and some that I was able to work with him. I would have gotten so much out of these things if I had been there earlier. It did seem as if I had to do things so that I was always a bit of an outsider....

This story is very personal, yet the experiences so unique, and yet so human, that I wanted to share even these dark parts of my process with my Apprenticeship, even as it draws to a close. I do not want to embarrass him, but, one can learn from even the seeming mistakes of one's Teachers. As long as I can come out on the other side of this stronger, and not still feeling paranoid that he got possessed by some evil force....

The more I thought of the Funeral idea, it seemed destined, as the last journey I had was very clearly suggesting I do it. For the journey was of being stuck in a tomb for ages, not able to really die, and yet wanting to die, almost suicidally, and to find release to go back to the stars and one's true community and people. That seemed to be a picture of sitting in the grave pit in the Shaman's backyard to symbolize my "dying" or a part of my life "dying," and waiting till dawn to come out to a new life, as a resurrected being. That would solve the being stuck for centuries in a tomb feeling.. And, my watching the Mayan Calendar on the wall also suggested the other side of that journey, the feeling of doom for the world, or the watching of the ages pass, and looking at the omens and stories told in the Calendar. The Calendar itself was a Mandala, in Jungian terminology. It signified a sense of wholeness and completion, or at least the need for such. The Dragon that landed on top of it was a good omen for completion as well, as it was the Shaman's symbol, and perhaps now a new shamanic helper for me. And even the feelings of despair at waiting with no response for centuries, and the feelings of abandonment were important, as they needed to be worked through for my transition to a new birth to take effect. Even that one simple depressing journey still had such power to teach and guide me in my process.

I was getting so much out of my journeys that it was a shame to stop them, as I felt I was tapping into layers of reality not just my own. Hopefully, one day I could learn to journey as well without my Teacher. I was hoping that he was taking me up on an idea I had that he should make up a CD that was like the induction of his journey session, so that I could do it at home from the CD and imagine I was still working with him in person. It should last an hour for a good long journey. He said he wanted to do it, and I also felt it would be great to have my own clients buy one so they could work on their own, too. That way I would not feel so abandoned, as I could journey almost as well on my own. Only without the loving person to hear my story when

I came out of it....

So, now I had as my task, planning my Funeral Ceremony, and setting with the Shaman a date for it. I had such a sense of peace when I had decided to do it, and got a sense that I should choose a day in which I would come out to my new life as a Cancer. That meant it had to be done in July before the 23rd. I also hoped that if I were lucky I could also have the Pleiades visible at the time of my ceremony, as that felt important for some energetic reason. But I was not sure when that was. Maybe it would happen by synchronicity.

I asked the Shaman to see if he could find me a new Medicine Name for my new life, the second birth in my life as Karen Degenhart, in this body. And after coming out of the grave pit, I hoped for a naming ceremony to give me this new name. It might become one of several I was already using, or it could become a dominant one for my new self. In any case, it would be representative of the results of my work with this Teacher, the Shaman in my book MEDICINE JOURNEYS: A SHAMANIC DESTINY, and perhaps it would be used on this book I am now writing as well.

The color of light blue was also influencing me, and perhaps was a new energy to come into my life. I also felt that Spirit would give me Power from doing the Funeral Ceremony. It was something I had to do. As for The Corn Farmer's idea to be wary of the Shaman using my energy or draining me, perhaps that was true in the sense that I had to let go of him some to gain more of my own power, now. I was too obsessed with him and needed to focus on my own spiritual work more. One has to graduate sometimes beyond ones teachers, whether it is easy to let go or not. 5/28/01

I also later got the idea to have a purpose for my ceremony beyond just doing it as mini-vision quest for closure, from reading a Shaman's Drum article, about a Lakota Yuwipi healing ceremony. It came to me that perhaps I could pray for a ceremony that I could do as a white person that might be similar, but not the same, as the ones the Native American's do for healing purposes. I would not aim to be a Yuwipi person, but there was a ceremony that was similar, but not involving the medicine person being wrapped up in a blanket and tied up, to be unwrapped by the spirits. The Lowanpi is a lesser but still powerful healing ceremony, that can be used for various purposes. It still calls in the spirits for healing. I thought I might pray for insight into how to do some similar kind of healing meeting or ceremony, and in general to have the spirits bless me with the power to do my shamanic work. This idea inspired me.

But, meanwhile, I was still uneasy and anxious about what this closure and ending of my Apprenticeship meant for my relationship with my Shaman friend. Even if I was no longer a student or "client", coming to him for journey sessions, I hoped we could meet sometimes to share things, or even perhaps to do some kind of groups together. I kept panicking about whether I was losing him or not by this change in our relationship.

Finally, he sent me an e-mail to ease my mind, saying that we would always be connected, and that he would gladly work with me on different projects after the graduation ceremony! That re-assured me for about a week, but after I had not been able to get a response from him re setting up our next meeting to discuss the ceremony or set a date for it, I started to get upset again. I was highly sensitive about this closure issue. I felt like he was ignoring my e-mails as a sort of behavioral technique, or just wanted to get rid of me, now.

CHAPTER FOUR:
PLANNING MY FUNERAL AND JOURNEY THIRTEEN:
VISION OF THE LIBRARY OF ALEXANDRIA

On June 4 the Shaman's e-mail had said we would meet soon to plan my Funeral Ceremony, but by June 12th, nothing had yet been set up. I had a dream that portrayed my anxious feelings about this lack of communication: "The Shaman is giving a lecture somewhere. He sees me there with a black back pack that has spoiling fruit in it, like strawberries and cherries."

I must have dozed off at work on my night shift job when I had this dream. I got more weird feelings during the night shift that night...like I was dropping into the darkness of uncertainty. I began to realize how badly I felt toward my Teacher, not only for his sudden wish to terminate my journey work with him, but even more for the unreliable way he communicated with me. He would send an e-mail of hope, that soon he would get back to me, and soon we could meet, and then eight days or more would go by, and the month of June was about half over, with no response to my many e-mails trying to set up an appointment and a date for my Funeral Ceremony, as I knew there were few free days in July in which our schedules might have matched to do it. I was anxious to get some closure on that. Yet, I also felt like a pest to e-mail him every day, asking if he had his new work schedule yet, so we could plan anything, and yet no response. I tried calling him, and got only the answer machine, and then was fretting that I might have to do it on a weekend, in which case I would have to take time off work and arrange a schedule switch with some co-worker. Since I worked weekends, that would be hard to do, also.

I would finally get to the point that I would be furious with him for ignoring me and my communications so much. Of course, he would never call me, for some reason. I was a real "back burner" issue now, I felt. It even felt like it could be a passive aggressive thing on his part to not get back to me. So, I felt hurt, abandoned, and sometimes even paranoid--as if I could not trust his word for anything anymore.

Of course, while I was going through all this, he was just "busy" and not responding to e-mails. That's what I found out later. So, I was over-reacting, to some extent. I was still nervous about "graduating" to this next level, as it was not really clear what this next level really would look like. It was supposed to be a rebirth, but was really a step into the unknown.

Meanwhile, as the Shaman pulled back his energetic involvement with me for this termination closure, my old boyfriend's energy moved back into my life again. I had decided we were broken up, yet he never completely went away. He dated other women without finding what he wanted, or getting the response he wanted from them.

Then, I had problems with my apartment not allowing pets, and I had to move my cats up to his rugged, mountain home to dispel a risk of being evicted. I had to come up to his home to check on my "babies." Luckily, Summer was coming, and it was more fun to visit the mountain where he lived. Not wanting to get sucked into any old negative patterns, I still allowed myself to visit him more frequently again. But I wasn't getting into anything too committed, as he tended to drain my energy, taking me away from my interests and shaman work. He wanted me to go out and market his business ideas, instead, even when there was no guaranteed or immediate money in it. I needed more time before I could re-consider being as focused on Don as I had once been, but we were still good friends.

Finally, the Shaman e-mailed me and we arranged a date to meet to plan my Funeral ceremony, the graduation ceremony for my apprenticeship with him. I came by June 19th in the evening. I had been mad at him earlier for not getting back to me very soon, but now I was calm and just glad to get to see him again. I shared some new books on shamanic topics I was reading, and gave him some gifts, and even a bit of cash. I asked if we could do one more journey, and he said we could. I wanted to have a different ending from the depressing journey I had last, now that I knew we were ending the journey process.

We also managed to pick a date for my Funeral ceremony that should work for us both. July 11th, in the evening. He wanted me to come the night before and do some digging in the grave, to get it ready, and feel like I am digging my own grave. I planned to pick some sage to put in the bottom of the pit, to be more like a Native American vision quest, and for spiritual protection. I could also leave some sweats or a blanket in the pit, so I could take off the nice outfit I will have on just before going into the grave, and be more comfortable.

I also planned to fast July 11th, perhaps even from the night before. But I would allow myself to drink some fluids for this quest, so I could do a pipe ceremony and be able to speak a few words about my Apprenticeship with the Shaman, and not be too dehydrated if it was hot out. I also planned to play some taped music, at some point, maybe before the ceremony's start, or between the pipe ceremony and while I am getting ready to be laying in state like a corpse, so people can have some last words with me.

I was planning most of this myself, I told the Shaman, but I asked him to do a naming ceremony the next morning when I came out of the grave, with a new Medicine Name that Spirit might inspire him to give me. And he said he had to conduct my Funeral. I guess I could not get out of the funeral image of this death-rebirth ceremony, even if I was doing it differently by being alive for a while to greet people and do the pipe ceremony, first.

I also planned to change a former vision quest staff I already had by adding a snake to it, to portray what I learned about the serpent/dragon symbol in mythology all around the

42

world, and how it relates to visions of DNA, as well as the Kundalini awakening process.

I then put together the outfit to wear that night and when laying in state. I choose a white dress, and with it to wear a fancy black and white beaded necklace that looks Egyptian, which was given to me by The Corn Farmer, my Hopi-Mexican spiritual advisor friend. I will wear my silver Eye of Horus with it, and some moccasins. In my hair will be two small eagle feathers, one of which was given to me from doing a vision quest with Lakota Ted Phelps. I will look like a mixture of Egyptian and Native American. I will carry a small purse that has a fake leopard design on in, since I often had a leopard in my journeys. On my breast I will hold a large eagle feather given to me by Floyd Hand, Heyoka Medicine Man, in one hand, and a large crystal in the other. In the small purse I will carry a silver medallion version of the Aztec/Mayan Calendar which had belonged to my stepmother, a crystal given to me by my Mom, Janet Doty, something of my Dad's, and Kleenex or a glasses case to protect my glasses when I take them off in the pit. I will have on some silver Native American style beaded earrings, also. It was getting fun to plan the details of my Funeral.

I also wanted to display some portraits of myself, some samples of my art work and mosaics, as well as to have some of the books I have written on display. Perhaps my sacred pipe that had been awakened by Sun Bear would also lay near my body.

JOURNEY THIRTEEN:
DISCOVERING THE LIBRARY AT ALEXANDRIA

Thirteen is the number of the Death card in the Tarot deck, so it seemed appropriate that the last journey of my apprenticeship was the thirteenth one. I did this whole apprenticeship with only thirteen journeys. From these thirteen journeys I wrote a book and started another one with the story of my apprenticeship.

This last journey started with a scene of palm trees and an old expensive car that was large, and grey with white walled tires. I felt I was in Egypt, possibly near where Alexandria would have been, and that a group or conference of important people, leaders and the wealthy, were meeting from all over the world. They came to decide what to do about an important archeological discovery that had been made in 1929. Or perhaps the meeting was in 1929, hence the old car. They could also have been discussing some world problem. Perhaps a remnant of the Library of Alexandria had been discovered. I felt a sense of evil that scared me, because many secrets were being kept from the world by the decisions of this group.

I moved through time to 1945, when my Teacher was born, and then to 1954, when I was born. I saw that he was a little boy about nine years old when I was born.

Then I saw a coffin and candles, which were the funeral of my Dad's real mother, who died just after he was born. She died of a goiter that could not at that time be operated on because she was pregnant with my Dad, and they chose to save the life of the unborn child, instead of her's. She died soon after my Dad was born, and he was raised by aunts and then a stepmother, when his dad remarried. There was something interesting about the DNA of his real mother, she was a free spirit, a gypsy kind

44

of person. At least that was a feeling I was getting.

Then I saw my Dad as a little boy, and saw him get older. He walked with me some, and I knew he was a soul mate, too, just like I felt the Shaman was. A soul mate can be someone you have known from all different kinds of relationships, not just a lover or husband and wife. It can be brother-sister, dad-child, mother-child, friends, cousins, and so on. Anything, really. Teacher/ mentor, and student, whatever. Even karmic ones who give each other trouble can turn up as soul mates to work out some karma, or make "restitution." I got the word "restitution" at some point in my journey, but had no idea what it referred to. It could have related to this secret conference, to some relationships issue, or some karma I was completing.

I saw a Star of David, and felt some ancient connection to Christ, or the line of David, but I wondered if the Jews used that symbol way back then.

Then, I remembered, that there was definitely some connection between the Grail and Egypt! I only remembered this as I was writing this up in my journal. I kept being taken back to Egypt, and seeing palm trees, though I did not see the Pyramids, thought they could have been in the area. I was not sure.

Toward the end of my journey, I saw some tall columns, and walked along a covered sidewalk that went around the outside of the large building. The air was humid and there was greenery around this pathway--it was not like a desert there. I felt a lush feeling, as I walked along this sheltered path amidst the tall pillars, and saw that a spotted leopard was at my right side, as I walked. From behind, I saw a person walking with a leopard at his or her side, and saw that I might have been the person. I did not even care what the sex of the person was. Perhaps androgynous. The leopard was a protector and companion.

Then, I knew that this was the Library of Alexandria, that had later been destroyed. It was still there in the shamanic world and I could go there for information. It had information from as far back as Atlantis at one time, and knowledge of other ancient and world cultures-- perhaps even information about extraterrestrial involvement in our planet's history, and about many ancient wisdom teachings. I felt so peaceful there, and just kept walking around the building. I didn't go in or even see a book, but just knew the knowledge was there, that I could access it if I needed to.

At one point, I felt that Carl Jung was there, or had been there, doing some research. People from all times came to this library for knowledge and wisdom, and it still exists in this other timeless realm.

During the journey, I cried some at various losses and emotional thoughts. I felt close to the Shaman again, after having been irritated at him before, and even paranoid for some reason that he was abandoning me, after my apprenticeship was over. But, now I knew he was my true friend, and always would be. I felt that perhaps I was afraid that I had abandoned him in some past life, and therefore I felt afraid of being abandoned in return, out of a guilt based fear. I felt, also, that he could have been involved with the Library of Alexandria, too, whether in a past life connection, or in the timeless spirit realm. He would make a good librarian, or keeper of the timeless mysteries, I thought. Perhaps I, too, had worked there.

Later, as I sat up and tried to tell what I then remembered of my journey, I took his hands in mine and cried some, saying he was my friend, and I just kept being afraid of losing him, for some reason. I tried to say I was sorry for something I might have done that was my fault, that maybe I had left him and felt guilty about it. I could tell that he forgave me for what ever it was. He said that we would be connected for a long time, and that I had done a good job with my journeys. I wiped my tears and he got some sage and osha to smudge me with to close me down after the journey session. He handed me my glasses, and we were done.

I said that I was still not real clear on what our connection was other than the clues I already had in past journeys, but I kept feeling there was more to know. He said that it was like in the book, THE RETURN OF MERLIN, by Chopra, that we were probably part of a Committee that meets every so often, over various lifetimes. He said that book was like his life. I had tried to read it once and had to return it to the library, but I now thought I should try reading it again, since it was like his life so much. I might get more out of it this time.

I had completed my Apprenticeship in thirteen journeys, and soon would have my final "Funeral" ceremony, going into a grave overnight. Thirteen is the number of the Death card in the Tarot, and I was going to die and be reborn, and get a new Medicine Name from the Shaman at the end of the ceremony when I came out of the grave the next morning.

We had finally picked a date that would work for both our schedules. Then he said I had to come the evening before to "dig my grave." I had to get the feeling of digging my own grave, and clean it out, in case it had snakes or anything in it, he said! That would be July 10th, after he got home from work. And July 11th, I would fast all day, and come early enough to further prepare and set up things. People would arrive at 6pm or so. I would greet them, being still alive, and say a few words about my apprenticeship, before doing a pipe ceremony, with the Native American Pipe that Sun Bear had awakened for me to be a personal pipe. I would now share it more as a ceremonial pipe, at least for that occasion. I will invite some new acquaintances as well as what few friends I have.

I wanted to play some taped music at some point, a tune from Jesus Christ Superstar, a tune called, "In the Air tonight," by Phil Collins, a tune from "The Police" called "Every Breath You Take," a Santana tune with the words about the "Monster under the bed," and a Blue Oyster Cult song that Don introduced me to, about Men in Black, UFO's and ending with "take me away...." I think I will start with, "In the Air Tonight."

After the short talk and Pipe ceremony, I would read a poem I wrote, and then have to take a break to lay in state, like a dead person, as I mentioned earlier. People could say last words to me if they wanted to. Then, the Shaman would lead me to my grave. Perhaps some more words would be said over my grave. I might get my Teacher to read another of my poems, called "Epitaph," over my grave.

Then at dawn on July 12th, I'll get a new birthdate to influence the rest of my life in this body, and a new Medicine Name from the Shaman. Re-born July 12, 2001. Numerologically, that adds up to: 7+12+2+1, or 19+2+1=22. 2+2=4. By this coincidental way of adding it up, I have a Master number of 22, and a reduced number of four. It sounds ok. I think it will work. And I will have a Cancer Sun sign. By another coincidence, July 12 is also the birthday of my friend Marsha. How weird. We can celebrate together. And Carl Jung was born a Cancer as well.

6/20/2001

CHAPTER FIVE:
"THE RETURN OF MERLIN"
AND MY FUNERAL

For several weeks leading up to my Funeral Vision Quest Ceremony, I was reading the book my teacher had recommended, THE RETURN OF MERLIN, by Deepak Chopra. My teacher had said that book was, "like my life," so I wanted to finally know why he often referred to this book.

The story was based on the idea that people who had lived in the time of Camelot and King Arthur, and his murder by Mordred, Arthur's evil illegitimate son, had reincarnated in our time, with no conscious memory of who they had been in the past. Yet, circumstances were drawing them together in the same battle of good and evil, with the reincarnation of the evil wizard Mordred. Merlin supposedly never dies, but he can also go in and out of time frames, and also can manipulate the past and the future, so he would gradually try to change the outcome of the past battle that had defeated King Arthur. In some magical way, this also could help the future to become more healed in our century, as more and more people awakened to spirit and peace.

But the battle waged in our time, with children as reincarnated knights, a policeman as Arthur, and so on. The evil force was adept at manipulating things so that people would suddenly fall in love with someone, not knowing that either it was a lover form the past, or a spell put on them to ruin some other relationship. Evil had subtle ways of interfering with things, so that no one was aware of the extent of its influence over them. People who were about to marry, suddenly broke up over some irrational argument, or were seduced, even raped, secretly, by evil forces, or led into destructive relationships. Death, self-destruction, or madness could even be the result.

For the two weeks prior to my ceremony, I also had weird coincidences happen at my job, which got me in trouble, unexpectedly, because some things got out of hand with the adolescents I worked with. They loved me, but I was supposed to discipline them more. The very day I was supposed to go over in the evening to "dig my grave" and bring some things to setup for my funeral parlor scene, I was depressed and in tears most of the day from coming off a staff meeting at work that morning (after working a night shift) in which it was mentioned that I had to set limits more with the kids, or could lose my job. I was quite depressed by this, yet I had no chance to even express it when I saw the Shaman, as his wife was there visiting with us, and offering me a last meal before my fast. No one knew how messed up I felt. I wondered if my life had really changed, or if my shaman training had done any good, after all, especially if I were to fail at another job, after only 4 $\frac{1}{2}$ months there. I had to suffer my doubts about graduating as a shaman in silence, within myself. I wondered if I could pull off doing the Pipe ceremony and short talk about my shamanic training , the next night. I felt like a charlatan, a fake....

I also had a couple of dreams about some evil force attacking me, even in the guise of my Teacher. July 6th, I dreamed: "First I drive to a road that is now boarded up, like it was some top secret installation. I cannot go there now. It suggests Danger. So, instead I take a nearby side road that is still open, though it looks rough and perhaps sandy, and difficult to navigate. Then the main part of the dream starts. I am in a different home, a condo some where else when I go to the door, and on the inside of the door there appears an indent that is like a face. It gets larger as I look. It is then like a mask mold, and I think of a mask that my Shaman friend had made from such a mold. I look at the growing indented face closely to see if it looks like the mask he had made of his face or not. Then, I see other, smaller faces around it, also forming in the door, like other spirit faces forming as indents in the door. Then, I remembered seeing some guy in the hallway, who was a new spiritual teacher who appeared out of no where, supposedly. I felt he was shadowy, and possibly dangerous. Then, some evil force is trying to hurt me. Things transform dangerously, like in some cartoon. A wire turns into a sharp pointed thing that is trying to wrap around or cut me. Suddenly it grows longer and sharper. Then somehow I trip and knock over a can of gasoline. I am stumbling around and fear a match or spark will ignite it, and start a bad fire. It is very dangerous and things are out of control, as I am being manipulated by some force to be clumsy like this. I see that the gasoline will seep into the carpet so that danger won't go away easily. I wake up, partly out of fear, and also to remember this dream. My consciousness of remembering it started with seeing the face mask in the door, which woke me so I remembered this dream." I think this dream was a premonition of a battle with evil forces, that was to come.

Another dream around this time was that I was attacked by a big, black panther--my Teacher's totem-- the same cat he had faced, and made peace with, to become a shaman, himself. I was able to hold down it's paws and tame it enough that it was no longer dangerous.

It seemed that for me, a modern battle with subtle evil forces was at work. It was intensifying for my ceremony of Death/Rebirth.

The day before the actual Death/Rebirth Funeral Ceremony, I had come off an overnight shift at my job with mentally ill adolescents feeling quite depressed over something that I had mistakenly allowed to happen on my shift, which was discussed at a staff meeting that morning. I felt my job was at risk, or at least my self-esteem had been shaken quite a bit. I had visions of being unemployed again, just when I was supposed to be graduating as a shaman. A lot of buttons were being pushed from past failures. I was quite depressed, and had been crying on and off all that day, except for taking a nap for a while.

I arrived at 6pm at the Shaman's home with a bunch of things to use in my Funeral Parlor Scene, such as paintings I have done, mosaics I have made, some books and LAPIS journals I had written and self-published, some star shaped candles, and a large crystal and an eagle feather I had planned to hold as a corpse.

I was supposed to dig in the grave for about an hour to prepare it for use the next night, and to get the feeling of digging my own grave. A thunderstorm started and it rained heavily so long that we set up the Funeral Parlor Scene in the house first. I ate some dinner with them, and finally just before dark, the rain stopped, so I could do some digging. It was quite muddy, but I dug and shaped the bottom of the grave for an hour and 20 minutes, or more. It was quite humid from the rain. My teacher brought a light so I could keep digging when it got dark.

Finally, it was nearly 10pm, and they wanted to go out and get some snacks for the Funeral the next night, and I had to stop digging. The physical activity of the digging was what I needed to ground me, and get me out of my depression. It also worked out well to dig in the dark, as it was cooler than it would have been to dig the next hot summer day in the light, which would also be harder as I would be fasting then.

As the Shaman's wife was there and we had a lot of setting up to do, I did not get a chance to even tell the Shaman I had this job problem that was depressing me so much. It wouldn't be a popular conversation topic, and I was embarrassed to have another job problem come up, just when it had seemed my job was stable. That seemed to be part of the evil attack I was experiencing for my Funeral Vision Quest experience.

The next day I was supposed to fast. I started my fast after the meal they gave me on July 10th, a Tuesday evening. On Wednesday July 11th, I drank fluids only. Bit of carrot juice and mostly water, as it was a hot summer day, and I did not want to get dehydrated.

I had a lot of things to do on Wednesday. I had to gather up my sleeping bag, some sweats to wear in the grave so I would not mess up the white dress I was going to wear earlier, and go pick some more sage that I wanted to throw into the bottom of the grave. I had to make sure I had my Indian Pipe, camera, and other miscellaneous things.

It felt strange fasting for a vision quest while doing normal, daily chores, or gathering sage. I would feel like I should stop for a bite to eat, then remember I was fasting. In previous Vision Quests, I was isolated in the wilderness where there was no food or water, so it was different. He had said this was an Initiation, but it was also more of a symbol of the end of our work together, and a symbol of a level of accomplishment in my growth as a shaman.

My teacher had said to come at about 5:15pm to plan how to schedule events of the evening. He was just getting home from work then, as I went out to my truck close to 5:30pm to bring back a pillow and camping mat that he did not want me to use in the grave (too comfy for a vision quest.) Just then a guest pulled up. That distracted the process some more, as the guest was early. He was a person involved in the UFO Disclosure Project, who also belonged to the Rosicrucians (AMORC version.) I did not know him well, but told him I'd buy a copy of Steven Greer's book on the Disclosure Project, so that enticed him to come. After calling his wife to see whether he should stay longer or not, he elected to stay on for the ceremony to put me into the grave. I had wanted to talk to him some more, but was too busy setting things up and greeting others as they arrived. The CSETI Disclosure Project guy was named Don, and so was my boyfriend named Don. My Don came soon with his video and digital camera, which kept him busy (not getting very good shots, however,) so that no one thought to use my 35mm camera.... So I got few decent shots of this experience, and the video was too

53

short and dark, for the most part.

After it seemed that everyone had arrived by 7pm, I started the proceedings with a Pipe Ceremony, using the Indian Pipe I have that was awakened by Sun Bear. Though I had never studied with Sun Bear, I had lucked out meeting him at a weekend workshop, where I bought myself a Pipe, and someone had told me I had to have it awakened by a Medicine Man before using it. So I got Sun Bear to do so, and he said some prayers over it for me. As I walked afterward to put the pipe into my truck, there was a small rumble of thunder! A first clue that the Thunder Beings were connected to me, and that I was to become somewhat Heyoka (the Lakota Contrary or clown.)

After I did the pipe ceremony, (doing some of the ceremony backwards, naturally), I elected to read a poem I had written in high school, called "The End Stirred." It had some symbolic parallels with my present situation, as I was ending my apprenticeship with my shaman teacher, as the poem was about a favorite teacher moving away at the end of the school year. The poem contained coincidental symbols of a dragon, which was my current teacher's symbol. There were some lines I really liked in the poem. I will re-print it here. In a strange way it seemed to predict things that were about to happen now, thirty years or so later! It sort of fit the mood of the end of my Apprenticeship.

THE END STIRRED

The end stirred, through papers
Blowing about us as we sat on the grass.
School papers, hitting us and clinging.
Peel them away, and again returning.
And us in the center with the High Priestess
And the Wheel, a broken wand,
And a sharp deal on a farm down South.

54

Here the wind swirled the garbage,
And it clung and made clear its existence.
The end stirred the beginning un-manifest,
Still at its hidden rest.
Leaves sprout from the wand,
But wither in the heat. There are no roots;
It is disconnected.... Hands bringing gifts
From nowhere. Beware. We're still there.
He prefers his humble log cabin,
Not a prison here.
Tall towers swirling in mid air.
Tears to smear, and exercises on mind and spirit
Teach me to sit, transcend transcendences,
Open new eyes, write pink melancholy poetry...
Riding and being tested on worldly economics.
Back and forth, past injured birds,
Through cold raindrops, into the sunset,
The silence, the music, of another life to come....

The Stranger and his Dragons passes me by,
Unseeing, in his blue-van wagon. Uncaring.
New adventures approaching young spotted spiders
To teach them to unmake their webs.
I am left to knit my thoughts and memories
Into dreams, unseen. Complicated etherical feathers,
Oceans of emotion to spill out into golden cups
Of wine, distilled.... Here, we're known
As we know nothing, and connect nothing,
With so many clues, sophisticated musing,
That vanishes into distant stars,
Veiled by violet-blue stars.
Now black birds fly,
Silently flitting and specking the sky.
Up into the heights where the air is thin,
And the breathing is slight,

Small dark wings stretch and beat,
Straining toward flight....

Below are papers, swirling and blowing helplessly,
Catching and clinging, suffocating desires
And entangled strings, burying the dead
On the lawn beneath a year's labor...
It's pollution of words and numbers and answers
To meaningless disconnected questions.
Gone with the faces. Gone with the days,
And the time, and the treasure.
Gone with the Dragons, and wise mystic sayings.
Gone is the knowledge which rippled
The waters of the heart. It is common, even petty.

Fragile feathers of words flutter and trail
Against the dead sound of the rotting ground....
Watching the black birds seek the sun,
Round yellow sun, pinned against the sky.
Dark specks barely moving,
Sensing the density of the mind,
And the hollowness of the time.
Move along. Where wheels turn
The Traveler finds new spiders,
And weaves webs of horror–
Horror because of possession.
Spirits, spirits, Here I am,
As one looking in, and considering
Outer space, and other exotic places,
Sitting on the crossroads, burden put aside,
Resting. From the Quest.
Fractioning infinity. Centering.
Knowing and growing put aside
Until the tide returns again....

Karen Degenhart

First published in 1972 in EDDA, Homewood-Flossmoor High School's literary magazine. Later published in DARK NIGHT WHERE ANGELS TREAD, in 1979, by myself.

After this, I planned to share some examples of the journeys I did with the Shaman. I thought I had more time than I did, so just as I was starting to share journey three, the Shaman told me I only had two more minutes left! I ended with the time in Greece where I had to kill myself by jumping off a cliff, to escape a worse fate from the Romans, when the Temples at Delphi were being closed down due to new laws to promote Christianity as the only religion. After this journey I found out the incident really happened, as priestesses of the Temple of Athena, located at the Delphi complex, jumped off a cliff to escape torture and rape by the Romans, who were on their way. I felt we took a drug to make it easier. Details on all this are in my previous book, MEDICINE JOURNEYS: A SHAMANIC DESTINY.

Then, the Shaman had everyone leave the room, and he told me, "Now you are dead, so you cannot talk to the living, or speak to anyone." Just after he said that there was a big rumble of thunder! It thundered a lot that evening, but there was no downpour this time (luckily, or the grave would have been a pool of mud.) I was asking my thunder being helpers to keep it from a heavy rain for my Quest, and it worked. Other areas of Denver got a downpour. Only a small drizzle occurred, on and off, during the night, so hardly any rain, but LOTS of thunder. Heyoka power.

Next, I was to "lay in state" in the darkened room, in the Funeral Parlor Setting we had set up the night before. I laid on the cushions, surrounded by my art work, mosaics, and self-published books, holding a large crystal in my right hand, and a large eagle feather in my left, over my breast. I wore a white dress, with a colored sash that had Native American figures on it, beige moccasins, a black and white beaded necklace that looked Egyptian, silver beaded earrings, and an eye of Horus necklace, over the beaded necklace. I had in my hair two small eagle feathers I had received from two sources. One was from a vision quest I had done with Ted Phelps, and one was a gift from a friend, the first eagle feather I had ever received. The two eagle feathers were tied into my hair with a medicine wheel, made by Ted Phelps' wife at the time. So my outfit had an Egyptian, Native American theme.

Then for 45 minutes people could come in and say their good-byes to me, as if I were dead. It was easier to lay calmly than I thought it would be. The Shaman had smudged me and it put me into a trance. It was interesting what people would say to me. I felt honored by it. One person made me make a smile when he said, "She looks as if she could still be breathing." That cracked me up, as I was still breathing.

After this, time was up, as it was almost sunset, so the Shaman came in and told me to put on my sweats (as I wanted to get out of the white dress for the night in the grave.) But he could not find them, and since I was not allowed to speak, I could not tell him where I last had seen them. I knew they were still in the Funeral Parlor Room, but had forgotten where I put them, as the black sweat outfit was hard to spot in the darkened room.

So, the Shaman went out to look and see if I had already put them in the grave, like I had originally thought. While looking, he found a small flash light I had left there in a plastic bag with some Kleenex, a t-shirt, an eyeglass case, and a plastic container to pee in, should I have to go during the night. He brought out the flash light and showed the group in the kitchen, saying, " I didn't find her sweats, but I found this, which is a no-no." They all laughed. (People told me later about this.) Once in the grave, I noticed it was missing, when I went to pee, and wanted to see better what I was doing in the dark. I was glad he

58

had found it, though, as I felt he should have searched my stuff, anyway.

Then, apparently, he also looked in my truck for the sweats, with Don's help, as he has a key. He would not let me talk, but I think I spoke by mistake saying they were in the room I was still in, some where. Suddenly, he found them in the funeral room, and said I had 2 or 3 minutes to change. He wanted me in the grave by exactly 8:28pm, what ever the papers said was sunset or sundown.

Then, he led me by the hand outside to the grave. I had on black sweat pants, and a black sweatshirt with some gold and silver abstract designs on it, like lightening or spirit lines. But, I still had on my yellow/beige moccasins. So, I had on the Heyoka colors of black and yellow. I climbed down into the grave and the Shaman told me to lay so my head was away from where the people were standing. He kept the wooden plank cover open while he read a few words, and my Don said a few words, and a couple of people sang songs that I did not recognize. I had spent a lot of time preparing a cassette tape of music I wanted to hear at my funeral, but it never got played.

It was starting to sprinkle rain, so all I could think while laying there was that I did not want to get rained on just before they closed the grave. I remember a drop falling onto my glasses, which were still on. I had my eyes closed. All I could think when the songs were going was, "Hurry up, and close the top! I don't want to get rained on."

Someone threw some rose petals, or maybe it was dirt, onto me, and then the top was closed. Since it could rain, they also covered it with a tarp, so it would not get as wet inside. I had thrown in some sage I had picked to lay on, on top of the Styrofoam bottom, and the bag of items I had left there (minus the flashlight.) After I was in the grave, they went in to drum and party some more.

It was then dark and quiet, except for suburban traffic sounds, kind of muffled. It was dark in the grave, except for some light I could see through the tarp, around the edges at the top, between the soil and some boards that supported the board covering.

My first test was that it was really hot. It was humid and the tarp must have held in the heat well. So, I was too hot in my sweats. Yet, since it was dark, I was still worried about bugs, worms, snakes, a mouse or other critter startling me, so I got into my sleeping bag for protection.

That was way too hot, so I took off my sweat pants and put on the t-shirt I had, luckily, left in the plastic bag. I peed to settle in for the night. I noticed the flashlight missing. Then I got into the sleeping bag in only my underwear, and t-shirt. But, every now and then I would be a little scared. Mainly because the Shaman had been so scared in his Grave experience, talking of worms all over the place. But, nothing scarey happened to me at all.

I moved around different ways, sat up, lay down, prayed, sang, quoted lines from that poem I had read, and so on. I used sage to comfort me and cool me. I could not sleep as it was so hot. I tried laying in different positions.

Once, I asked if there were any spirits there, and suddenly a big, loud, chunk of dirt fell down from the side into the pit!

Later in the night, I did sleep some, and dreamed that the Shaman was in a room next to the grave, down at the same level, only separated by a wooden door or wall, when suddenly the wall broke open, and I knew the Shaman was on the other side of it. This bothered me, as I thought he might have heard my prayers, some of which might have mentioned him. I prayed to keep some relationship with him, even though my Apprenticeship was over, for example. But, I was also kind of glad to know he was close by.

There was a moment when I thought it was light in the grave, and I felt maybe I was going to see in the dark. But it was still not clear enough to see much. It was more of a sensation of a brightness, or of my third eye opening.

When sunrise came, I heard some noises, maybe a door shut, and then the Shaman and a strange woman, not anyone I knew, were opening the grave cover to help me out. I was now re-born. We went inside in the kitchen, and I was given some juice to drink. I looked at the clock, and it was around 5:37am or so. I knew the papers had said 5:42am was sunrise that morning. So I had been taken out of the grave several minutes early. But, it was already getting light.

The Shaman went into the bathroom, while I and the woman who had been with him talked a bit. I will call her Kay here, but that is not her real name. She worked with the Shaman as a teacher at the facility for problem kids where he worked as a nurse. He had been a psychiatric nurse for a long time before this job. I remembered her coming last to my Pipe ceremony, and wondered who she was, as I had not invited her. My friend Margie was not there for my Rebirth, which surprised me, as I had thought she was going to be there all night to support me and be there in the morning for my Rebirth and Naming Ceremony. Coincidently, her real birthday is the same as the new one I could claim for this Rebirth date.

While drinking some orange juice to break my fast, I asked Kay how she happened to come to this event, and she said that she worked with the Shaman, and he had shown her his short story about his own Funeral Ceremony experience, which got her interested in seeing mine. She made some comment that he might have overslept if she had not awakened him, in which case I would have missed coming out of the grave at sunrise. I thought that it was strange that my teacher could not wake himself, when he was supposed to be managing my Funeral Vision Quest. As we were talking, she mentioned having to go get her shoes. For some reason she had left them outside, but not right by the back door. Near my grave, perhaps? It may have still been a bit muddy from the rain of the last two nights.

When Kay gave me a hug, I felt an unusual energy from her, a kind of healing energy that reminded me of a dream I had in

61

April in which a woman was meeting my Shaman friend for lunch outside on a bench by a pond. The woman in the dream called herself Inanna, the Goddess, and looked similar to Kay, except may have been thinner in the dream. Both Kay and the dream Goddess had blonde hair. I thought when I hugged her that perhaps she was the one in my dream, and figured that they did sometimes have lunch together, since they worked together....

Later, we went outside so I could take a few photos to remember this event, and have a picture of the Shaman and myself. That's when I saw the tent that had been set up after I went in the grave, for my Teacher to sleep in to be near me for support during the night. Suddenly, I realized that my dream of him being close by in a near-by room where he could possibly even hear my prayers was true! So, Kay must have had to wake him as he nearly overslept in this tent. She apparently had gone home but come back very early to see me get out of the grave. I still felt kind of sad that a stranger had to help me with my rebirth, and that no real friend could stay for this part. But, it was a week day morning, and actually my Shaman friend had to work later that day, and had worked the day before. I only had days off in mid week, and it was a new job, so I did not get any paid time off yet. I did my grave digging on a Tuesday night, my Funeral and Burial on a Wednesday night, and my Rebirth on a Thursday morning. While I was in the grave, the guests who had come had a drumming session, and more of a party, staying a while to talk, but not real late, for the same reason.

While the Shaman made me some eggs and toast for breakfast, I opened some gifts for my new birthday which some of the guests had left. During this time, Kay also volunteered that the Shaman was getting his short story about his Funeral experience published. I was surprised that he had not told me about this. After further questioning, I realized that it had not yet been accepted, but that he was going to send it out for publication. Then I wanted to see the final version, as I had only seen a few pages of it earlier. He gave me a copy to keep.

My Rebirth-Day was July 12th, at approximately 5:42am (or a few minutes before), which was sunrise, by the newspaper. I opened my few gifts and cards. I never got birthday gifts anymore, as both my Dad and stepmother are dead, and my boyfriend never gave me anything. Sometimes my Mom, who lives in Australia, might send me some money or gift, though. I rarely got anything for Christmas now, for the same reasons, though sometimes something from family members now living in Australia, or from a Swedish friend. It is weird that all my family, and a rare good friend, are so far away. So, even the small gifts I got for this were special: A rattle made of deer hooves, a buffalo statue, an Indian beaded mandala necklace, a Tibetan smokey quartz crystal, a dream catcher, and from the Shaman, a hematite pentagram (which is a star in a circle.) That is the only gift he ever gave me, but I had given him many gifts as payment for my shamanic journey sessions.

Then, the Shaman led me into the room where my funeral bed was still set up. He handed me a short, heavy sword to hold in my right hand, which looked like it had some lapis stone in the handle. Then, he read from a card he had designed on the computer, which said, "You who are nameless have traveled a long and at times torturous path. In your dying you have suffered, but have endured as well. In doing so you have arrived at another station along the journey. It is at this station that you begin anew. *** By the dawn of the morning light, you will be, from this time forward, known as Morning Star, one that shines even in the light of day. Do you accept this naming as well as the responsibilities, duties, burdens, and joys of this calling of Shaman?" It was signed, "Warmest Regards, Antonio." He read this and I responded, saying, "I do." My new Medicine Name was Morning Star. I was now an Initiated Shaman.

I later got a copy of what was read by the Shaman over my grave, as he had it printed on a card, which also used a neat drawing by one of my kids at work, of a skull with a dragon. The card said, "Funeral Services for Karen Degenhart," "Death is the only wise advisor that we have. Whenever we feel that everything is going wrong and you're about to be annihilated, turn to your death and ask if that is so. Your death will tell you that you're wrong...your death will tell you, 'I haven't touched you yet.'" Don Juan, <u>Journey to Ixtlan</u>, Carlos Castaneda."

"Thank you for being here. We are here for many reasons, the least of all is to say good-bye. Times like this cause us to reflect on the nature of our own existence. Life is fleeting. These events provide us the opportunity to stop and take notice of what life means to us. In this instance, Karen, a guiding light in a difficult process, has served as an inspiration. Her creativity and persistence were impressive. She was like a multi-faceted diamond with her books, her art, her spirituality, and her heart. There will never be another like her. Her gifts were many and remain as beacons in the world. It was my good fortune to have known her. She will be missed." "July 11, 2001."

The real meaning of "The Return of Merlin" and the battle of good and evil was revealed soon after this, and is a story which will be very difficult to tell. My first task as a Shaman was to face a Shadow which I never expected. This was my hardest test, and yet I was only able to share it in confidence with a couple of friends. My relationship with my Teacher changed after this ceremony in a totally unexpected way.

After my ceremony, I was yanked back to reality by circumstances, kept my night shift job with the adolescents, and became closer again with my boyfriend. I lost some connection with the mystical shamanic realm, but found a new life, which was functioning better than my previous one. It still had its challenges, but I could feel transformation in the air. I was not quite the same person ever again after this experience. (Written October 10, 2001)

CHAPTER SIX:
THE REVELATION OF SECRETS

I had finished reading THE RETURN OF MERLIN just before my Funeral ceremony. Ironically, I had been reading this book the very night that some of the kids I was working with got into some sneaky homosexual behaviors, and that was why I later got into trouble for not watching them better. Since they were in a facility, there were state laws against sexual contact. I was still green in dealing with the wiles of kids with hormones. Ironically, one of the kids who got me in trouble, was later to play a role that I never would have expected. He had a connection with Merlin, too. It was almost as if the book was coming true in my life, with people I knew.

The first thing that happened after my Funeral ceremony that was strange was when my lady friend, who I will call Margie, who was supposed to have stayed to morning to welcome me out of the grave, was not there, and a strange woman was there instead. Margie later e-mailed me that she had some uncomfortable feelings about staying, especially since she might be the only one staying overnight, because she was afraid of sexual advances from my Teacher!

After having made that confession, as we talked more on the phone the next day, I found out more of her story. I had invited Margie to attend the Shaman's 2000 Fall Equinox drumming party, where she met my Teacher and got to talk with him, giving him her card to make a connection. She kind of wanted a shamanic teacher, too. He soon called her up and invited her on a lunch date. She expected to just be friends or talk about shamanism, or maybe with luck he would accept her as an apprentice, too. But, instead, he came on to her like he was looking for a sexual relationship. Luckily, she knew he was married, because I had told her, for he did not act married. She asked, "What about your wife?" He acted shocked that she knew he was married, and then made some comment about not having a good sexual relationship with his wife, as an excuse. My friend felt like a piece of meat, and was insulted. She said she never wanted to see him again, but promised not to say anything about this to anyone. She did keep her secret for months, while I was seeing the Shaman for my "treatment" and shamanic training/apprenticeship. Only after my Funeral and my training was over, did she feel she had to confess this information to me, to get it off her heart, and to protect me, by letting me know about this other side of my Teacher.

She did not want me to tell anyone else, but I was too upset to keep the secret. I was really upset at my Teacher, because I really loved him, and I remembered being so desperate to see him in the Fall, and after a session in October, did not get to see him again until January. I really suffered during that time, having troubles with my boyfriend, job failures, lack of money, and holiday blues. And yet, he had time to date my best friend behind my back! I felt almost like a betrayed wife, myself. At least a betrayed apprentice. And that was why Margie could not stay for my rebirth and naming ceremony the next morning after my Funeral.

I freaked out, not able to handle both the termination with my Teacher, and finding out he was propositioning my best friend behind the scenes. I myself still had a crush on him, as my Teacher, and I thought, friend. My biggest fear was losing his friendship after my work with him was over, now symbolized by the Funeral ceremony. I was not totally innocent, as I was attracted to him, too. But he was smart enough to not come right out and proposition me.

I had thought that being an Apprentice was a special relationship with my Teacher, and that it might become a more equal relationship over time. I enjoyed hugging him and an occasional brief kiss after a session, but I knew he was married and had no illusions about how available he was. I only thought some friendship might be possible once I graduated. I guess our boundaries were getting a little sloppy once I was nearing the end of my training, and had completed the book I had written and published about my earlier journeys and apprenticeship. But, I thought we were pretty much following the rules, and would never have dreamed that he was actively going after other women during this time. I somehow thought I knew him, and that he would not do anything like that.

I next made the mistake of telling him in some e-mails that I knew about his date with Margie, and what had transpired. I was angry and hurt about this, since for some reason I thought being an Apprentice was a special relationship, but it was not as special as he thought he could have with someone else, even my best friend. I could have kept the secret and played like I did not know anything, but I was hurting too much.

The next thing that happened put the nail in the coffin of my happy friendship with my Teacher. A few days after my Funeral ceremony, another woman who had come to my Funeral, but did not stay overnight, wanted to visit me and find out more about my experience. She was a long time friend of the Shaman, as well as his only other Apprentice who had done the Funeral ceremony. I had made a cryptic comment in an e-mail to her that something had happened after my ceremony was over that upset me. I did not plan to tell her all about Margie's comment, but when this person, who I will call Nancy, came over, she drew it out of me by telling me that he was known to do special touches and other things to kind of seduce women, and that she had noticed him doing it some in this group she was teaching with him. She further confessed that she had an affair with him some years ago, and she told me many details of her experience of loving him, that sounded like my own inner story. I did not have a physical affair like she did, but I felt the same feelings almost as if I had experienced a kind of love affair, perhaps in the aethers.... We both felt he was like God, sometimes, or a saint, something more than human person. It is hard to fathom the feelings of divine union one can feel, even if it is not acted out physically, with a person who has true shamanic abilities. It feels like Divine Love and it seems totally OK, no matter what temptations may arise. After having an affair like this, women still would be in love with him, and thus protect his secret, even if he hurt them and broke it off. I could tell this, as I later learned of even more affairs he had, and could see a pattern.

So, why am I not protecting him, since I loved him so much, too? The main thing that got to me was that he started to blame me for the truths I had found out from others! And, he said in an e-mail that he would not have anything to do with me because I allowed this information to get out of hand, and that he would even deny that I had been his Apprentice! Even after I had gone in debt printing my book that honored my work with him, and dedicated it to him!

I thought this might blow over, but he never could deal with the confusion and hurt and anger that I expressed in some e-mails after these revelations, and accused me of being the trouble maker who was doing this to hurt people (bullshit!), and I could not heal from it without some better communication than a couple of e-mails.

He then went into a three month retreat, after my ceremony, and also said he was quitting being a Shaman. He reported in the last e-mail I ever got from him that he even had cut his long hair and was not communicating with the outside world for this time. He would fluctuate from being very cruel, saying I was forbidden to use his name or say I was an Apprentice, to saying good by and good luck and may God be with you, but it did not heal the pain I was in, as now I could not trust anything about him, anymore. Then I never heard from him again. And our relationship was apparently over. But the Karma wasn't, as I was still in pain from being rejected by the most significant helping relationship in all my life, and felt very hurt and betrayed, and spiritually wounded by this.

It got worse when, even months later, I heard from another source, that he would pretend he had never heard of me! While my books were for sale in the same store where he sometimes would go for drumming meetings! Anyone could go to the shelves and see the story I had put my heart into to honor my work with him. And he denied even knowing me. That seemed to clinch for me that I was now dealing with some kind of evil force, that I would never have expected from this kind person who I had previously adored, and trusted my life to.

Now, the irony and mystery continued. The very kid who had gotten me in trouble at my job, and nearly fired, was one who I later happened to talk to about shamanism. He said he was part Seneca and when I had told him about doing a shamanic Funeral death/rebirth ceremony, he said he had done one, too. His was more serious, and in a real coffin, he said. He was very intelligent, and knew a lot of interesting things about shamanism, and many foreign languages. He knew a lot about Merlin, and said that Merlin had been at his birth, and that Merlin lived backwards in time, just like it says in that book I had read. He implied that I had some kind of connection with the King Arthur story as well, much like the characters in that book who were reincarnations of people from the past. I had often thought of my Teacher as a kind of modern King Arthur.

When I told this kid about my Teacher, he said that he felt psychically that my Teacher was going to find out soon that he had brain cancer, and that he would not live long! This kid then said he knew a woman who he thought also knew my Teacher some years ago, and that he would put me in touch with her, as she might have some information that I should know about my Teacher. I don't remember her name, but I will call her Raven.

Raven did e-mail me, so I knew he was not making it up that she existed and knew my Teacher. She knew of my being upset at finding out about his secret life of seducing women, even though he is married. He has been doing it for years, unashamedly, according to her. I only talked about this with

69

other shamanic people, in an attempt to understand and heal myself. The information that Raven gave me was that she had been my Teacher's teacher, and she was the one who introduced him to the Funeral ceremony in the first place, as she is full-blooded Seneca. She had done a similar ceremony, herself.

(By the way, I later read somewhere that many Native Americans had become Masons, and that this death/rebirth ceremony was originally a ceremony to become a Master Mason!)

The fact that my Teacher had learned his teachings from Raven who knew his secrets, and called him evil, really demystified him for me. She really warned me about him. She is the one who has now told me in an e-mail that when she brought up my name, he pretended not to even know me! Thanks a lot, dear Teacher....

But, then I wondered about her. Why was my Teacher still talking with Raven, if she secretly felt he was evil? Wouldn't he know that she did not really like him, now? Was he so stupid that he did not know she was telling me these discrediting things behind his back? I guessed that he had called her because she is a shaman, who had been his teacher, and he needed healing for his supposed cancer. She kept saying he did not have long to live. I have not met her in person yet, and only communicated by e-mails. So, for now, I cannot be sure what is the complete truth, but some of it seems real. And all of it is sad. 2/22/02

CHAPTER SEVEN:
IN LIMBO AGAIN

I later thought, it is ironical that my Teacher, who I had called the Shaman, went to this Seneca female shaman for help with his illness, when I am the one who might actually be able to help him if he has cancer--for my boyfriend Don has actually helped to cure several people of cancer with Essiac.. Essiac is a recipe based on an old Indian herbal healing potion. Governments are afraid it really works, and it is outlawed in Australia. It may also be outlawed, or at least suppressed, here in the States. We know places where we can get the ingredients, as some are harder to find in the quantities needed for a decent batch of Essiac. We both have the recipe.

I occasionally sent an e-mail to my Teacher about how I was struggling with finding out that he was saying he didn't even know me! He was really scared of my penchant for telling the truth, I guess. But he never responded to anything I would e-mail him, even my offer to help him with the Essiac recipe, if he needed it.

At the same time that I found out about his ultimate betrayal of my spirit and love for him and our work together, I was also unemployed. My job with the kids in the Residential Treatment Center, at which I was then working on the easier night shift, had ended at the end of January 2002 because the facility closed down. It was actually privately owned by a psychiatrist, and kept going in the red due to over staffing, and poor management. So, the best paying, full time job I ever had, that I might have been able to tolerate for a while, had ended.

I was getting tired of it, anyway. I had to work every weekend, Friday, Saturday, Sunday, Monday nights, from 10pm to 8am. I had done this schedule for 9 months and for a couple months before that on the swing shift, still with weekend hours.

I was getting kind of tired all the time from lack of proper sleep, and slept too much on my days off to make up for it. Don also seemed to hate this job, since I could never visit him on weekends, anymore, while I was working there.

I am writing this a month to the day after my last shift on that job. I felt relieved when it ended, so I could take a break from work, and get back on a normal sleep schedule. But I was also confused, because job hunting is such a liminal process, and a quirk of fate could lead me into a whole new career, or a meaningless dead end job. I did not feel much sense of control or direction. This is partly because even though I am educated as a therapist, I am not licensed, so the best jobs are out of reach. And yet I was burned out on all the direct care jobs I had done over the years, working with DD, MI, CMI, the elderly, and now most recently adolescents. I was really tired of it all, yet did not have the correct office or computer skills to excel in anything else.

Or maybe I could learn some of those things and try to get more skills, but that still takes time and money to do. Worse, I was now spoiled by that easy night job, where I could watch TV and read, or even sometimes take a short, light nap, and get paid $10.00 an hour for it. A hundred dollars a night. Then I had Tuesday, Wednesday, Thursday, and Friday until 10pm off every week! Of course, some of that time I spent sleeping, especially Tuesday after working for four nights, so I wasted much of that day sleeping to catch up. I could not imagine holding down a full time job, 9 to 5, Monday through Friday! I had been using my shamanic abilities to get easier jobs to get by on, I guess.

Some unemployment money should come eventually, but once it runs out, would I have a job I liked that paid enough to live on? Or to catch up on some of my debt? By now I had a lot of debt. About a third of it was money I borrowed to buy this stock Don kept saying was going to go up and make us rich, but it was worth a quarter of what I paid for it, now. Another large debt amount was from printing up my book, MEDICINE JOURNEYS: A SHAMANIC DESTINY, which I wrote to share my work with my Teacher, and to honor him, though I just called him "the Shaman" in the story, to be less specific about his identity. (Lucky for him, now!) I also used some of this credit debt to buy an old 4wd Subaru, that got good mileage, for safely getting to work in the winter and for visiting Don easier in his isolated mountain home. And the Subaru needed some repairs after I got it. I also had charged some dental work a couple years ago, and who knows what else. I borrowed from one credit card to pay off another, using lower interest rates, but often paying high transfer fees. By February 2002, I owed around $17,000.! I had never even taken home that much money from a job in a year! But, I kept hoping the stock would go up so I could pay it off. I had decided to take more risks, but I wanted to be able to pay off my debts, and keep good credit.

My shamanic practice was fizzling out, since the broken relationship with my Teacher had broken my spirit to do it, anymore. Just thinking about trying to do a drumming ceremony for journeys reminded me of how bad I felt about my Teacher's betrayal. I needed to work through this issue to find, in fact, my purpose and any real joy again. I even wondered if I should make some kind of professional complaint against him, for the misconduct that I knew about. But, all I really wanted was to know he was still a friend who could offer even some limited support for me and my shamanic work. He was only human, after all, and I could put some of his affairs in perspective. I could have been seduced into something, myself. But, for him to betray the relationship, the love I felt for him and from him, was the ultimate curse put on my soul. I was afraid to call him and even confront him about any of it. It felt like he would be mean and hurt me more. Or pretend not to even know me. (That hurt the most.)

The other side of things was that he might be ill or dying, so then none of this inner turmoil mattered. Even his betrayal

73

did not really matter, except in a very sad, ironic way, because once he was dead, who would care one way or another what he had said about me to a few people who might ask? I knew I was his Apprentice, and my books talk openly about his influence on my life, which was good until after my Funeral ceremony, after which the truth started to come out. And, quite a few other people also knew I had been his Apprentice. Those who had attended my ceremony knew. Those who read my book knew, for how could I make up what was my real life? What I had learned from my journeys was still potent in my life, in a strange way, like a memory that you can't get out of your mind. His wife even knew me. His deception would not be able to live on after his death. My work with him, and even the love we had was real at one time. Being his Apprentice meant having a friend to share some things with, and some support from having had such a good experience with him. It was supposed to be special and a good memory. Now it was trashed. I was still hurting. I could not believe he also now ignored me, as well as denied knowing me.

There was also no longer a cult-like community of shamans, mostly women, coming to drumming meetings at his home. The value of those meetings had been trashed, even if he had any more of them, for even if I were invited, I now knew the secret, the elephant in the room that no one wanted to mention-- that several of the women in the room had affairs with him, and I loved him, too, but never actually had an affair with him. And his wife did not know most of it. Maybe none of it.

Being his Apprentice meant nothing without his love, yet that was already gone, and would be forever unreachable after his death. But, I think as for the prestige it would give me, or anyone, he had an exaggerated opinion of himself in that area. I think that was partly why he was dying. He had been misusing his power. He once had said he would CHOOSE to die at age 75, to just starve and dehydrate himself until he could leave his body behind. But Death had another plan--it seems....

I am writing this without conclusive proof that the Seneca

Shaman woman is telling the truth about his terminal illness. I will write this book as it happens, however, and let events unfold naturally, as then my story will follow the natural truth of the flow of real life, as that will be stranger than fiction, no doubt.

The information and insights I got from my journey work with him was so conclusive for me that it does not matter WHO helped me to find it out! It stands by itself, and so does my continual process of discovery related to that same body of knowledge and insight. The only clue that came from my Teacher was his use of the Dragon motif. The Dragon/Serpent motif guided me in unexpected ways on my journey.

The day I wrote this past section I had gone to see the movie, "Dragonfly," starring Kevin Costner. This movie synchronistically dealt with death and dying issues, and with levels of consciousness leading to death, and with other shamanic realities. Somehow, I gained a sense of peace about the situation with my Teacher as I watched this movie. I decided to send him one more e-mail, saying that if he would ask for help, I might be able to help him with the Essiac recipe, which is an Objiwa Indian recipe that has been said to cure cancer. In fact, my friend Don has made it and helped several people who either had cancer or might have. They all got better, or did not need surgery after all. But the Shaman has to ask for help. And, he has to be humble enough to approach me for it, otherwise, if he is ill, he might die....

But, he did not respond to that e-mail, ether. I thought maybe he was doomed to die, that his sins were killing him. I remembered saying to him after one of my last sessions, "Now that I have met you, there is nothing else to wait for," like meeting him was the culmination of my life, and now I could die in peace. But, in actuality, perhaps once HE MET ME there was nothing else he had to wait for. Now he could quit being a Shaman, or perhaps even die, because HE had to wait for ME, to complete a Karma between us. Unfortunately, that Karma may now be renewed again because of his denial of our relationship,

75

and thus hurting me again.

Even with this mis-communication and his potential death looming, I am able to go on with my writing, research, and spiritual path. I am deeply wounded, but still he has helped to Awaken me. No one can take that away. Even if I become dysfunctional in my career, I am more awakened then I was before we met. Sometimes being functional in this society is not all it's cracked up to be, anyway.

I admired the Shaman more than anyone because he seemed to take me on to help me out of a genuine sense of caring, yet now that I know about his secret life and shadow side, he won't even communicate with me by e-mail, and he tells other shamans he does not even know me. My only vindication is to keep on writing, writing the truth.

CHAPTER EIGHT:
ARE THERE ANY SHAMANS WITH INTEGRITY?

It is now toward the end of March 2002, two months after I lost my job, and so many people are out of work right now that I STILL have not gotten any unemployment money! Luckily, I have many credit cards and some savings left. I could possibly have a chance to get a job much like what I was doing, but in reality I was not sure I still wanted to work with troubled adolescents. There are a lot of jobs with adolescents, and many of them are budding criminals. That says something about our current society, I guess. So, since I am supposed to be getting unemployment funds, IF they get around to sending it before I run out of resources, I wanted to explore some other options, or if I did end up working with kids, I wanted to be a therapist, not a direct care worker any longer. I am 48 years old; I deserve a REAL job in my field of education before I die! Either that, or do something totally different that is more fun or pays better. So, every week I had to study the Sunday paper for leads, and sometimes get leads from the computer, and apply for jobs--all kinds of jobs. Therapist jobs, case manager jobs, mortgage originator jobs, forest ranger jobs, summer jobs with little kids in my town, apartment manager jobs, and so on. I did not know what I might be led to. I either wanted a better job in mental health, or something totally different. If I got desperate, I could apply for home care with the elderly, or another job with troubled kids. But I was not yet desperate.

After I sent some e-mails complaining to my Teacher for saying he did not know me, I figured he might have guessed how I heard that. Sure enough, my source, the Seneca Shamaness, perhaps suspecting that he figured it out that she was telling me things, withdrew her connection that barely happened, and said she was going out of town again. I began to distrust her as well. She did not have the integrity to let me meet her and find out who she is, yet she was trashing out my Teacher even more, telling me he had a long history of seducing women, mis-using his power. I figured they all were playing a game, and I was tired of it.

Then I found out that another Shamaness I knew, who had a metaphysical store which carried my books and crafts on consignment, had skipped town, apparently taking my things with her--unless I hear from her later or find her.... Apparently, things did not work out with her store and she owed money to people. (I later heard from her that she had been in a bad car accident, but I never got my things back.)

I refreshed my memory about other Shamans I had known. One had seduced me and given me a kind of VD. Another one had been my best friend and then invited another woman from Australia to help him supervise my Vision Quest, even though I had a crush on him. And he then wanted to marry her! (That did not work out for him, anyway, but it split us up, and I never saw him again.) One Medicine Woman I had known was also a friend. She betrayed me by stealing my other best friend, and taking her on as a student, and later deserting us both! Now, another one has skipped town with my property. And one that knew my Teacher's dark secrets cannot show her face to me, and stops communicating by e-mail. What am I to make of this? Shamanism attracts a lot of flakes and people who lack integrity. Or who like to live in some kind of illusion. Or, perhaps it is actually spiritually dangerous.

Ironically, while working with my Shaman, he seemed to act like he thought I should break up with Don, and in fact, for a while it seemed we were breaking up. But, as soon as I was done with my work with the Shaman, Don seemed to come back into my life again. But, I felt stronger after my work with the Shaman, and did not allow Don to manipulate me so much. I felt more independent. We were still like a couple who have separate places to live, but I have cheap rent and a lot of stuff, so it worked for me. I like a lot of time alone, too. In spite of some things Don has done to hurt me, we have lasted for over ten years now, in some kind of relationship, and I feel something steady from him that is just not there with these Shamanic characters. In the end, Don has more integrity, and I can appreciate that about him.

What seemed to be happening now was like a reversal of what had happened a year ago. I had started my new job a year ago, and now I was unemployed because the agency closed that department. I had a crush on my Teacher and Don was trying to date someone else. Now, Don and I are back together, and my Shamanic Teacher pretends he does not even know me, nor am I able to communicate with him. It is almost like I never met the Shaman. Things are back the way they were before I met him. I have Don in my life, at least part time, and I have no steady job. That is how things were before I started my Shamanic work with my Teacher. It is like I went through some strange cycle and am now back where I was. In a way, it doesn't make sense, except that I feel at a higher place in this spiral journey....

Years ago I left a liberal Protestant church, because they seemed so unsupportive of me and so political and not spiritual, so I took up Native American ways. At that time, the Christians I knew seemed to lack something. But, now I think the Shamans I have known are worse. There seems to be no refuge. I end up on a very individual path. There is no one out there who one can really trust to guide one. Or so it seems. I trusted the Shaman for a while, but that turned out to be an illusion, too. As I peel away all the illusions, it really HURTS, but after a while, I feel stronger. It is like now I can see through just about anything, at least I hope so, after all this....

CHAPTER NINE:
THE UNEMPLOYMENT VACATION

Now it is June 2002 and I am still unemployed. I have not tried really hard to get work, but I have had some significant interviews for jobs better than I have ever had salary wise, as I had vowed to myself to take only something that paid better and was a higher level job while I still had unemployment benefits. Once the benefits run out, I will have to take what ever I can get, again. But I did do enough work in my job hunt to wonder what I would do if I were really desperate for work and did not have any unemployment benefits? You can spin your wheels a lot without getting any responses in job hunting. My particular difficulty was that I had never really "broken in" to some nitch that people could peg me into, and so I was usually over educated but did not have the right experience for many jobs, and also now that Colorado had licensing for counselors, I was competing with those who were licensed, just by the grace that they had been able to jump through certain hoops and document their experiences and supervision to get licensed. I have years of varied experiences but did not have the right supervision that could now be easily documented. And I might even have to take some extra classes, to get Colorado licensure. My problem now was being middle aged and not having a clear cut career YET, and always trying to break into something that might develop into something. But now I was TIRED of the low paying jobs in mental health, that also had lousy hours. I wanted some kind of work that had a larger income potential, perhaps some kind of sales, or if I took a counselor job, a position with which I could work toward finally getting licensed. I could still have a private practice in Colorado without being licensed, but even that entailed now an additional class I should take for a

80

hundred dollars or so, and another $250. to register with the State. Luckily up until now the work I had been doing was Shamanic and Spiritual, but if I really wanted to do a more complete private practice I should pay these extra fees and sign up with the State. However, here I was unemployed and did not have a lot of money. So, what to do?

I was also attracted to Real Estate, another license that would cost money to get, and loan originating, just because it paid well. Maybe I could help people get loans to build "Kronos" homes with Don's building invention, too. I had no idea what I should try next, all I knew for sure what that my last job had soured me on working with mentally ill adolescents. So many of them now days are just criminals, and sociopaths. Most of the facilities hiring were more like prisons than anything else, and that was hard for me to be around. I am so empathic and psychic now days that it is hard to be around facilities of really messed up people. Thus I desire work that is more pleasant and upbeat. What I will end up taking next is still a mystery. My best hope is to do some kind of self-employment.....And I still hope maybe Don will get something going. I enjoy doing house plans for Kronos homes.   I'd like to have the money to be a Kronos builder, just doing one or two homes at a time, starting with my lot in Crestone. (Don later changed the name of his company to Cavity Wall Technology, but we still sometimes call it Kronos panels.)

I have been thinking of my Teacher, and in a way I now feel I was kind of crazy when I went through those journeys, yet they still have empowered me, in spite of him. I do wish that he might contact me sometime just to see how I am doing, but his silence either affirms his desire to wipe me out of his mind, or that he is dying.... By the end of this book, I hope to know for sure what is happening with him.

A year ago, I was planning my Funeral ceremony. I had no idea the trauma that was soon to be in store for me. Even now, I have a hard time marketing my last book that was mostly about

81

my Teacher and my apprenticeship with him. But it is still an important story. Those times were significant in themselves. And I also learned from other shamans, too. Sandra Ingerman at least still leaves memories with integrity. And I still e-mail the Australian woman who called herself then, "White Wolf." She is a good person on the shamanic path. But there are so many shamanic flakes who lack integrity. Be really careful. I guess to become really strong spiritually, one may have to be betrayed by nearly everyone one trusts and needs, like Christ was....

As far as the job hunt and unemployment goes, I am just taking one day at a time, and enjoying being out of work with pay for so long. I am able to get by on around $900. a month due to my still low rent, even though my credit card debt is still pretty high. It is summer weather now in Colorado and a nice time to be out of work. Except we have bad fires this summer. They will go down in history....06/18/02

CHAPTER TEN:
THE WHIRL WIND UNLEASHED

For months I tried to suppress my pain at feeling betrayed by my shamanic teacher, also feeling that he was punishing me for loving him and wanting to be a friend. I loved him but I hadn't had an affair with him like other women had. But his refusal to communicate with me made me blame myself. He was blackmailing me, saying in an e-mail that I had to stop talking about his secret affairs or he would have nothing to do with me, and would say he did not know me. I was not supposed to use his name as my teacher!

For a while I also gave up on e-mailing the Seneca woman shaman who had leaked to me the information about his many affairs. She had insisted they were not just affairs, but "horror stories" of emotional and sexual abuse, to both his and her students. She would drop some bombshell like this and then go out of the country for a while, doing initiations in England or Scotland, and I would not hear from her for a while. It was like people kept telling me about my teacher's secret sins and then abandoning me to stew with the information. But it was a hot summer and I was also distracted by my unemployment.

But, come July and August 2002, and I started to relive the pain and confusion over what happened after my funeral ceremony with the Shaman. This was what psychology calls the "anniversary" effect, which calls up unresolved feelings from an event when that date or time of year comes around again. Since my Funeral was in July, 2001, when July 2002 came around, I began to process the whole event again. I remembered the exact date of a mean e-mail he had sent to me, the one in which he said he would pretend not to even know me, and have nothing to do with me, if I did not stop talking about him and his affairs. It was a couple weeks after my funeral ceremony. I was just devastated by this comment from him. Even though he later made a more conciliatory remark in a later e-mail, it could not erase what he had said previously, that hurt me so deeply. Remember, I thought he was some kind of saint, or an old friend from another life, and I also felt we were friends forever, and connected at a very deep level, like Twin Souls. I was in love with him, in a way, but more. A cosmic love. Eternal. This just could not be happening that he could turn cold like that.

This was also like a therapeutic relationship and so the wound was deep, as if my therapist had cursed me. This was horrible. One of the worse things to ever happen to me, and it blew my mind and soul. I was abandoned and betrayed by someone I had trusted completely with my soul. I wondered if I could sue him for professional misconduct. I did not know what to do.

Just after my final ceremony, he had gone into seclusion for three months, a kind of shamanic purification thing, and was not going to see anyone socially. I wondered if he had found out he was ill, and wanted the time to heal himself. The Seneca shaman woman had said in e-mails that he was dying of brain cancer, and did not have long to live. Still, I could not prove it, and was afraid to call him up to find out.

There is another weird and far out coincidence in this story. Through my job with the troubled adolescents, I met a young man who was also into shamanism. We talked some and found out we had each done a kind of Funeral ceremony. He was part Seneca and had done it with some elders as an Initiation. He used a real coffin for his, he said. He was even partly buried in it. As I shared some about my ceremony, he began to realize that he might know of my teacher. He talked to the Seneca woman shaman (Raven) and then supposedly she had a message for me about my teacher. Apparently, SHE had been my teacher's teacher in the matter of this funeral ceremony! She was younger than him, but had been his teacher. So, before she e-mailed me later, she sent a message to me via my adolescent client. The client was supposed to warn me about my teacher still having affairs, and that he was ill with brain cancer and would get his karma soon enough.

Well, you can imagine how this made me feel. I was torn. My Teacher was both more evil than I had thought, but also now dying as well. And I was no longer communicating with him, or getting any responses to my e-mails, so I felt really abandoned, upset, betrayed, and confused. It was also confusing that Raven, the woman shaman, was being sort of secretive, and would not give me her complete name and identity. At certain points, I wondered if they were all conspiring to play with my head. But on the other hand, it all seemed to fit the other information I had been finding out from other sources who I trusted to be authentic.

Yet, everyone who told me these horrible things, abandoned me after telling me the information (except for my friend Margie.) One woman who had told me she had a nine month affair with him, was so upset when I told her he had been making moves on my best girlfriend, she would not talk to me, or anyone connected with my teacher. She then disconnected with me as well, since I had been one of his students, too. She was teaching a class with him and told him she would finish it up without him. He had been making moves on women in their joint class, too, but she had not believed it for sure till I told her my story. And all this when he was still broken up from their previous affair, saying he could not continue that affair due to being a married man!

Now, it was as if there was a curse on ME for letting the information get out. Even over a year later, I wrote to one of his former students to find out if he was ill or not, and I did not get a response from that person. Others blamed me for "gossiping," People who were still under his spell would not give me the time of day, yet I went from being one of his most talented apprentices to an outcast. This was a total collapse of a community, as well, for me.

When I would think about all this a year later, it was as if it had been a Cosmic set up of some kind, for it was as if I got that job, just so that just before they went out of business and closed down the facility for the kids, I was to find out from one of the kids about the faults of my teacher, and connect with the Seneca shaman woman, Raven, too. It was also a set up in that my girlfriend who had the advances from my teacher, finally confessed after my work with him was done. She was worried about whether to tell me or not, but since I sounded so enthusiastic and did not seem like he was approaching me, she held her tongue, because it was helping me to see him. I was not supposed to say anything, but when his other former apprentice, Nancy, learned I was upset about something I found out after my ceremony, she pried it out of me, and then she confessed her story. Then soon abandoned me herself.

I felt also more powerful as a shaman in that apparently I was the catalyst for this exposure to happen-- I, and my girlfriend who had confessed about his advances. I felt that he had been lured into a trap. The sad part is that he fell into the trap because of a good quality he had; he had compassion for me and wanted to help me out. I was his last apprentice and student. He had wanted to quit but took me on out of concern. I have heard that sometimes we are done in by our compassion. That seems wrong, but it was the trick to get him exposed in the end. Our best qualities can be used against us, by evil, or by justice, in this case. Karma.

All the thundering during my vision quest in the grave now made more sense. Heyoka powers were at work. A reversal occurred. A total reversal. I lost the most powerful friend I thought I ever would have, and my wonderful shamanic journeys and even the book I wrote about them was now tarnished. All around, a lot of relationships were destroyed. For a long time, I could not enjoy drumming and did not do any shamanic journeys, or take any clients. I was messed up for well over a year over this. It did not help that I was also out of work for such a long time, too.

As soon as I learned what I needed to learn, and made some e-mail connections with the shamanic woman Raven who had more to reveal to me, the facility I worked for decided to close down. That is so weird, as it was as if I was only there to learn this information, to get more reality and resolution (eventually) about my teacher, and my loss of his friendship.

The other side of this is that I felt traumatized so much that I had no desire to do a job like this again. There were too many negative associations. It was not just from this, but some other poor management problems on the job that discouraged me, too. But, I think I did help some kids there. I got laid off due to the facility closing down, so I qualified for unemployment, and got to live on unemployment for about 8 months. That was also a gift to me.

So, by August 2002, a little over a year after my Funeral Initiation ceremony, I was re-living my pain over my teacher's turning his back on me, and decided to e-mail the Seneca shaman woman again. Now she responded that my Teacher was so ill that he was living in a hospital, but the hospital had given up on him and wanted him to move out to a hospice! However, now his wife was divorcing him, so he could not go home. The Seneca shaman woman (Raven) said in an e-mail that she had offered to let him stay with her and to try to do some healing on him. Yet, she was the one who had been telling me all the horrible things he had done, apparently without him knowing that she was doing this behind his back. She told me via e-mail, but her communications to me were not very steady. I still had not met her or even talked to her on the phone.

Around the same time I am finding out that possibly my Shaman Teacher was dying, I was finally to receive a very special Native American pipe bowl from an elderly relative named John Degenhart. He had followed the Indian ways for much of his life, but I only found out a couple years ago from some e-mailings with his daughter, Debbie Degenhart. I actually picked it up at the post office on August `12th, 2002, a year and a month after

87

my "new 2nd birthday" of July 12th --my rebirth after the Funeral ceremony. Debbie has asthma and so did not care for the pipe tradition, but when she heard I was following Indian ways, she asked her Dad, John Degenhart, for permission to give the pipe bowl to me. Though he was frail and brain damaged from a car accident, he was aware enough to understand, and nodded yes. This pipe bowl I was to be given as a gift from John Degenhart had been a gift to John from none other than Lame Deer, John Fire Lame Deer, a now deceased but well known Lakota Medicine man! The stem had been lost or destroyed over the years, but the stem had been added by John. The bowl was the gift from Lame Deer to John.

The reason for this gift was that apparently Lame Deer had become friends with John Degenhart when John had been a minister on a reservation and helped the whites and Indians who lived in the area to get along better. Debbie says this happened in 1960. Well, I was 6 years old then. Lame Deer adopted John Degenhart and gave him the pipe bowl. John must have done a vision quest as well, as Debbie says she has a pin that was also a gift from Lame Deer to John Degenhart, that was a vision quest gift. It has beaver fur on it.

Debbie says that John had collected many Native American items over the years, and made many himself, in authentic ways, and had been given gifts, so that he had accumulated several hundred valuable items. She wanted to give most of them to the Smithsonian for their new Native American exhibit, but I don't know if that ever happened. She hoped to get me flown there if these items are put out, so that I can do a pipe ceremony with this pipe bowl (plus a stem I would add to it) for that event.

Strangely, Debbie had originally mailed this pipe bowl to me on September 10th, 2001, and after the events of September 11th, in which the Twin Towers, and more, were destroyed by the terrorists, the mail was in turmoil, and many large packages were searched. For some reason, they did not know what to make of a Native American pipe bowl. This valuable pipe was lost for a few weeks in the mail, before it finally came back to Debbie Degenhart, who had mailed it to me. She, then, was in her own turmoil, going through a divorce, and had to leave it in storage, not having money to send it again with the expensive insurance she felt it required. So, it ended up in storage for almost a year. She had to move around to get settled, and could not come back to get it for some time.

As my Shaman teacher was in his three month seclusion period until mid October, 2001, when the pipe was temporarily lost in the mail, I was still hurting over his rejection, but unresolved. A part of me still hoped to regain some friendship with him. However, he did not respond to e-mails during this period, either. So, I was left hanging, feeling he had already wounded me terribly in a couple e-mails he had sent, but I was sort of in disbelief as to the permanence of this. I think with what happened on September 11, 2001, and with the hurt and pain in me, and anger, also, toward my Shamanic Teacher, that the pipe knew it had to wait to get to me, to connect when this pain was not so immediate. It had first been mailed to me on September 10th! For a while we feared it could have been in mail on one of the crashed planes....

So it was around a year later, August 12, 2002, when I finally got this pipe bowl from John Degenhart by way of his daughter Debbie. The same day that I got the pipe bowl in the mail, I also got a letter from a Native American named Looks At Clouds. In his letter, as I had told him previously about how this "Lame Deer" pipe bowl would be coming to me, he warned me to really watch it, and not let just anyone even touch it. People could try to steal it, etc. I have to be really careful with it.

The "Lame Deer" pipe bowl came in a pipe bag made just for the bowl by John Degenhart, which was beaded and totally authentically made, in spite of the fact John is a white man of German stock. He even brain tanned his own hides. He found his own porcupine quills. He dyed things with natural dies. He copied the styles of authentic Native American items. It did not have a stem, so I would have to get a stem to smoke it and pray with it.

As I studied the bowl, which was a classic "Four Winds" style, I noticed some words scratched on the bottom of the bowl. I could not make it out at first. But finally I could tell it said, "Whirl Wind." I thought it might be the name of the maker of the pipe bowl, putting his name on it. I wrote to Debbie, who was without e-mail after her divorce. She wrote and called at various times and told me more of the story of this pipe. The word "Whirlwind" on it referred to an Iroquois Mask that had been blessed by this pipe in a three day ceremony! This mask was painted red and black, and had horse hair on it. This was the item Debbie planned to keep for herself out of her Dad's large collection of Native American items. (Later, I heard she had given it away, also.) So, now I had a Lakota pipe bowl that had blessed an Iroquois mask, in a three day ceremony. That is all she could tell me at the time. Maybe that is all I will find out....

This red catlinite pipestone bowl also had sort of a darker and lighter side to it, sort of like the mask's colors of red and black. And on the bottom of it is a "V" in a lighter colored part of the stone. A "V" like in Victory. Or it could look like animal horns. All this made me think that this pipe bowl was going to be very special, if only symbolically, in some way.

Before she moved to Missouri, I had shown a lady friend my special pipe bowl and the "Whirlwind" word on it. She then said she had just been reading in one of William Henry's books, a strange mention he made about a quote in President Bush's inaugural speech, about "an angel in the whirlwind." As if Bush knew there would be a "whirlwind" during his term of office, but that an angel would get us through it. As I find out more about this quote, I could add it to this book. I find it a strange synchronicity that this pipe is named Whirlwind, or connected with the Whirlwind mask, and that the pipe was first mailed out the day before September 11, and Bush is talking about whirlwinds in his speech. The pipe was, in a sense, loosed upon the world as it was being mailed, intended to get to me, the day before September 11. However, it was then delayed nine months by the events of September 11th, as it finally got to me August 12th, 2002. Eleven and Twelve are also the numbers significant in my Funeral Initiation ceremony. I "died" on July 11th, and came back on July 12th. It seemed to me that it might not be a coincidence that this pipe bowl was literally neglected, in storage, for years, and as soon as it came out of storage, intended to be used, the Whirlwind was set upon us, in the events of September 11th. However, I am not saying this pipe is negative. I think it is a tool meant to help fight the evils that have been unleashed upon the world since then. I think it is a tool for Victory, victory of the good. But, the Whirlwind could be now upon us, as the Ghost Dance religion predicted. Perhaps in wars, perhaps in Earth changes. In many ways, a Whirlwind is now upon us.

A further strange coincidence was a prediction made by the shamanic Seneca adolescent who I met at my job. He had said in a comment, that he had gotten a psychic impression about a coming "War of the Lance" to be unleashed upon the world, an unleashing of pure evil. This comment I wrote down in my journal, as having been made around September 3, 2001, just a matter of days before September 11. The War of the Lance...well, the planes were taken over with small knives.... He also had commented that he thought my Shamanic Teacher, was really Draconian. A draconian is sometimes thought to be a particular kind of alien, who are often more evil than good. This kid was not stupid, but he had a mental problem that required medication and he needed some space from his home environment. In fact, he had already written a book about shamanism, which he printed himself, and sold in a local store. He was just turning 18. He knew many languages since his parents were in the military and he lived in many parts of the world. He said he was of Seneca Royalty. And, he was also gay.

So this was my normal life--going to work and getting prophecies from a young shaman, that warned me of hard things about my Shamanic teacher, and predict September 11. All in a day's work for a shaman, I guess.

Later, I got an e-mail from this young man, as he was friends with the woman shaman, Raven, who had taken my Teacher in to heal him from his brain cancer, and the kid said that she could no longer e-mail me, as my Shamanic teacher had threatened to SUE her, as apparently he had found out by her e-mail address that she had been saying bad things about him to me, and others. So he left her care and vanished. That is, until one day sometime in October 2002, when someone else reported seeing him, and he later shared in an e-mail to that person that somehow I was to blame for him losing his job! I took that to mean that somehow all his affairs, and his Don Juan personality problem had gotten out (my fault?) and that he was fired. No, he did not say he lost his job, he had said to this person that he has lost his "career." So maybe he could never work as a nurse again. Especially in psychiatry or where kids were concerned. Maybe he lost his license. But, I was not the one to turn him in. Maybe it was that other apprentice, Nancy, who had also done the Funeral ceremony. She had been particularly disillusioned after finding out he was not reformed after breaking up the affair with her. "I am a married man," he had told her, and yet was seducing women in the class they were teaching together!

I had idealized him so much that I could not understand this side of him at all. When he abandoned me for finding out all this, I was devastated, as I have said. This was a real big lesson for me, and a test of some kind. I lucked out, as I had been as emotionally entangled with him as possible, but he did not manage to get so far with me, so I must have been protected. Now he blames me for his own undoing. Perhaps I feel more powerful as a shaman for that, but it was Spirit who set it up.

Yet, ironically, it was this man who has given me the name of Morning Star, and I still use it, as it is still my rebirth ceremony name, and has connections to some members of the Lame Deer family who were named that. So, I have carried a wound in my new self that constantly reminds me of this harmful experience. I have had to heal much of this in order to like this spirit name again. Perhaps another name will come for me someday, but Morning Star is very traditional and mythological. It has power in itself.   12/14/02

On August 31, 2002, I had a fight with my boyfriend and so was kind of depressed. I decided to make myself go to the Metaphysical Fair on September 2nd to cheer myself up. There was a talk by Skip Atwater on Remote Viewing. This was by donation only so I could afford it, though I was still unemployed. In this talk we did several experiences of remote viewing. I was very encouraged by my results from these. It really cheered me up, and made me start to believe in my psychic abilities again. Even my ability to do remote viewing and other psychic tasks had been wounded by the rejection by my teacher. I think I felt for a while that I could only do such deep consciousness journeys under his guidance. But, now I realized that he was just a facilitator, and that I could still do these kinds of things with my mind, and that I did not need him. My wounded soul had a sort of PTSD in which anything connected with things I did with my teacher held pain in them. Even going into my own psychic abilities and doing shamanic journeys had been associated with this pain. So, the thing that Skip Atwater's workshop did was to begin to heal me and free me from this association. I now knew that I could do remote viewing and psychic journeys based on my own abilities, not just with my shaman teacher.

I felt more whole from this experience. I was on the way to healing, but not quite there yet. 12/27/02

CHAPTER ELEVEN:
HE MUST BE DEAD

Believe it or not, it is NOW March 2007, as I write this new chapter to conclude this part of my story. I have been through a lot of other challenges and shamanaic tests since what I wrote in Chapter Ten. I will share those parts of my journey soon, but for now I want to conclude what I know of the fate of the Shaman.

By October 2005, I was living with Don again in the mountains. I was going to do some work helping seniors in their homes part time, and had to go down to the Denver area for training. On the way back from training, I was to pass by the street that my Shaman Teacher had lived on. I had never had the courage before this to even drive by his house. I had last seen him in July of 2001, and now it was October 2006. Five years had passed, so now I needed to drive by his house to see what it looked like. I had heard he was dying of brain cancer, and I kind of assumed he had died.

Strangely enough, as I drove down the street looking for his house (or former home), I at first could not see anything that could be it. I turned around at the end of the block and came back again by where it should be. It was all different now. The lush and overgrown lawn of wild plants was now like bare dirt or dead grass, and the tree that had covered the entry walk was gone as well. It was bare and barren looking now, but it had to be the same house, as this was a short block, and there was no way I could miss it if it were the same landscaping. It was obviously owned by someone new. But, it looked so dead now. Before, it was like a magical entrance into another world. I wondered if the new owners had filled in the "grave" hole in the back yard where the Funeral ceremonies had been done. I figured they probably had. This was strange to see. Indeed, it was as if an entrance to another world had been opened and I had fallen into it. Who would have guessed the strange coincidences and adventures I would have experienced from this house? It had been so magical, and now it looked less than ordinary, almost pathetic.

I had also never heard again from the young man or the shamanic woman Raven. Nor a clue about Nancy, his other apprentice, either. It was almost as if none of it had really existed, and yet it was part of one of the most powerfully positive AND negative combinations of experiences I have ever had. (March 24, 2007)

ABOUT THE AUTHOR

KAREN DEGENHART, MA. MDiv. PhD. has used several Medicine Names over the years. Her first one, Thunder Stone Dream Woman, she gave herself as a pen name for her first book . Joseph Rael once sent her a note with the name, Stone of Fire Spirit, on it, which seemed to be a spirit name. This name Karen thinks of as a secret name, and has not yet been used outwardly. Later names came and went as Karen went through phases of her growth. Ravenwolf was used on her last book, MEDICINE JOURNEYS: A SHAMANIC DESTINY, along with Thunder Stone Dream Woman. In THE WOUNDED SHAMAN, she received the Medicine Name, or Rebirth Name, from her Funeral Ceremony, of Morning Star. This name seems almost more archetypal than individual. Her Teacher had said it was the Star that was so bright it could be seen in the light of day. It is a Star of the Dawn: The dawning of a new world, and the death of the old.

Karen has a BA. In English, an MA. in Counseling, a MDiv. from Chicago Theological Seminary, and a PhD. in Pastoral (spiritual) counseling. She also has a certificate in Hypnotherapy. In spite of all this, Karen has lived in poverty and underemployment all her life. How is this? In America? Ha!

At this time, Karen lives in an off-the-grid home with her boyfriend, Don. It is cheaper to live this way, but it is not easy. It takes a lot of effort to keep wood stoves burning around the clock to keep warm. It takes a lot of work to go out to cut and get the wood, to split it, to move it around. Getting drifted in for weeks on end is frustrating. It is hard to hold down any job from this mountain home. It is tricky making sure that water from the well is pumped into the cistern and does not run out unexpectedly, especially during freezing weather. Getting mail and groceries can be challenging.

Karen currently is self-employed part time teaching arts and crafts projects, primarily Mosaics and Native American style crafts, adding more projects as she learns. Karen also plans to do more writing, as there is a book AFTER this one that needs to be written. She plans more promotion of her Counseling, Hypnotherapy, and Shamanic Journey Work, which she learned from her Shamanic Teacher. She hopes to produce some hypnosis CDs, and DVDs with Teachings she wishes to share.

99

CreateSpace Availability:

The Wounded Shaman
http:/createspace.com/3332323